THE REVIVED LIFE

Exploring the Glorious Freedom of
the Spirit's Cleansing, Enabling and Authority

Exploring the Glorious Freedom of
Divine Cleansing, Enabling and Authority

The
Revived
Life

JOHN R. VAN GELDEREN

FOREWORD BY RICHARD OWEN ROBERTS

CLC
PUBLICATIONS

The Revived Life
Published by CLC Publications

U.S.A.
P.O. Box 1449, Fort Washington, PA 19034

UNITED KINGDOM
CLC International (UK)
Unit 5, Glendale Avenue, Sandycroft, Flintshire, CH5 2QP

© 2012 John R. Van Gelderen
All rights reserved
This printing 2016

ISBN (paperback): 978-1-61958-009-1
ISBN (e-book): 978-1-61958-020-6

Unless otherwise noted, all Scripture quotations are from the Holy Bible,
King James Version.

Italics in Scripture quotations are the emphasis of the author.

DEDICATION:

To Mary Lynn

My faithful wife and companion on our journey
to know and experience Christ's life.

CONTENTS

FOREWORD

As a young man, I remember hearing a sermon on "The Three Deadly D's: Disappointment, Dissatisfaction, and Despair." Although the speaker's name was long ago forgotten, the heart of his message is still with me.

Disappointment with the Christian life is rampant today. This disappointment is clearly heard and seen in the murmuring, the complaining and the grievous unrest that is so popular and prevalent in today's church.

When disappointment is left uncured, it can easily lead to levels of dissatisfaction with both Christ and His Church that result in abandonment. Multitudes have already left the organized church. Unless they come quickly to repentance, they are soon likely to abandon Christ Himself. Disappointment with Christ has already led many back to the same evil practices from which they once claimed deliverance. Dissatisfaction has already reached such levels that we find little real distinction between the moral conduct of the church and that of the world.

Dissatisfaction, left unresolved, eventually leads to despair. In consequence, multitudes who still think themselves Christians have entertained an escapist mentality and hope that Christ will hurry back and save them from this mess. Others have simply given up hope and returned to their own fleshpots of Egypt.

The compromised lives of defeated Christians dot the landscape of the church everywhere you look. Observing this sad scene, one might unwisely suppose that Christ can only save believers from the penalty of sin, but has no power to save from sin itself.

Did the angel who confronted Joseph at the time he was struggling with being betrothed to a pregnant girl misspeak, saying, "Joseph, son of David, do not be afraid to take Mary as your wife; for that which has been conceived in her is of the Holy Spirit. And she will bear a son, and you shall call His name Jesus, for He will save His people from their sins"? Was He really speaking of Jesus saving people in their sins instead of from their sins? Or, was He suggesting that Jesus would save His people despite their sins? Or was He possibly suggesting that Jesus would save His people from the penalty of their sins while leaving them to struggle with their sins?

If Jesus saves His people from their sins, precisely as the angel said, why are there so many who call themselves "Christians" who are still trapped in their life of sin? Must that be their lot throughout life, or is there a way of escape for them?

There is a wonderful life of victory and joy in the finished work of Christ which is available to every true believer. John R. Van Gelderen's book *The Revived Life* makes that way of escape plain.

Read it with a hungry heart!

Read it with an open mind!

Read it in faith, believing!

Read it and rejoice in what the Holy Spirit does in empowering you to live the exchanged life in all its fullness and fruitfulness!

Richard Owen Roberts
International Awakening Ministries

ACKNOWLEDGMENTS

More than any other publisher at the present time, CLC Publications prints books for the deeper life, sometimes called the higher life, the victorious life, or the Spirit-filled life, but all of which address accessing and experiencing the very life of Jesus Christ. A special thanks to CLC director, Dave Almack, and the team at CLC for adding this volume as another twenty-first century articulation of the Christ-life truth; to senior editor, Dave Fessenden, for his enhancing editorial work; and the graphics designer David Montgomery, for yet another great cover design and layout. May the Lord, the Life Himself of the revived life truth, give life to all who read this volume.

1

THE LONGING SOUL
The Beginning of the Adventure to Freedom

For he satisfieth the longing soul, and filleth the hungry soul with goodness.
PSALM 107:9

Greater than any craving for food and water is the deep long-ing within the soul of many of God's children to be like Jesus—in a word, *to experience Christ's life.*

Over the centuries of time, multitudes have echoed Paul's words, the cry of the heart that epitomizes "the longing soul": "O wretched man that I am! who shall deliver me from the body of this death?" (Rom. 7:24). There is a deep agony of soul in the painful admission of one's wretched condition and the seeming prospect of inevitable defeat. Evidently, Paul had exhausted the possibilities of "What shall deliver me?" and found them all fu-tile. So he cried out, "*Who* shall deliver me?"

Our loving heavenly Father desires to satisfy the longing soul and to fill the hungry soul with goodness. Truly there is hope! Many saints from the past testify to this reality. The following examples demonstrate what can happen when ordinary people learn to access an extraordinary God.

13

The first testimony we consider is in a chapter entitled "The Darkest Hour" from the two-volume biography of Hudson Taylor (nineteenth century missionary to China):

> But "the heart knoweth its own bitterness," and the load Hudson Taylor was carrying was almost more than he could bear. It was not the work with all its difficulty and trial: when consciously in communion with the Lord these seemed light. It was not shortness of funds, nor anxiety about those dearest to him. It was just—himself: the unsatisfied longing of his heart; the inward struggle to abide in Christ; the frequent failure and disappointment.[1]

At that time Taylor began to read a series of articles on "the deeper spiritual life . . . the life of habitual victory over sin, the life that is in deep reality 'Not I, but Christ' for which [his heart] longed." His biographer writes, "To know *that* redemption, that love, in fuller measure was Mr. Taylor's deepest longing; but oh, how different were the actual experiences of his soul!" The pressures of the mission increased, and demanded so much of Hudson Taylor's time, yet, "oh, how deep the heart-hunger, in and through all else! *That* did not diminish."[2]

But in the providence of God, he received a letter from a colleague in the mission named McCarthy. God blessed the contents of this letter by illuminating a life-changing truth to Hudson Taylor. He wrote, "As I read, I saw it all. I looked to Jesus; and when I saw, oh, how joy flowed!"[3] This moment turned the tide. Hudson Taylor began to experience Christ's life in far greater measure.

The second account is that of Rosalind Goforth, a missionary to China with her husband Jonathan in the late nineteenth and early twentieth centuries. In the early years of their ministry in China, Rosalind overheard a conversation of Chinese workers. Unaware that she was on the other side of a thin wall, they talked about Rosalind. Admitting she obviously loved them and was a zealous worker, they begrudged her impatience and quick temper. Then one said, "If she only would live more what she preaches!" The remark cut deeply into Rosalind's heart and angered her, but she knew it was far too true. Grieved, she fled to her room knowing her life lacked usefulness if she could not even live Christ before the Chinese workers.[4]

A little later in their ministry at Changte, they had a house built. To dispel vicious rumors about the "foreign devils," they allowed their house to be an open house for weeks so the curious Chinese could investigate. Once when a small group of Chinese women entered, one exclaimed loudly, "Oh, these foreign devils, the smell of their home is unbearable!" Rosalind tells the story of her response in her autobiography *Climbing*:

> My temper rose in a flash and, turning on her with anger, I said, "How dare you speak like that? Leave the room!" The crowd, sensing a "storm," fled. I heard one say, "That foreign devil woman has a temper just like ours!"
>
> Now, I had not noticed that the door of my husband's study was ajar, nor did I know that he was inside, until, as the last woman disappeared, the door opened and he came forward, looking solemn and stern. "Rose, how could you forget yourself?" he said. "Do you realize that just one such incident may undo months of self-sacrificing, loving service?"
>
> "But Jonathan," I returned, "you don't know how she—"
>
> But he interrupted, "Yes, I do; I heard all. You certainly had reason to be annoyed; but were you *justified*, with all that is hanging in the balance and God's grace sufficient to keep you patient?"
>
> As he turned to re-enter his study, he said, "*All* I can say is *I am disappointed!*"
>
> Oh, how that last word cut me! I deserved it, yes, but, oh, I did so want to reach up to the high ideals he had. A tempestuous time followed alone in our inner room with my Lord.[5]

Rosalind longed for victory, but she did not know how to access it. Then in the providence of God, while at home on a furlough, she read a sermon on Galatians 2:20 by Charles Trumbull entitled "The Life that Wins." The Holy Spirit illuminated life-changing truth to her heart, the scales of hindrance fell off, her eyes were opened, and she began to experience Christ's life. The transformation continued. She writes:

> Many months (I forget just how long) had passed after our return to our Changte station when one evening one of our leading evangelists came in just when my husband was about to start for the street chapel. The evangelist showed plainly he wished to speak to my husband alone, so I left the room. When he had gone, I returned to find my husband standing by the table with a strange look on his face. He seemed deeply moved, yet glad. I exclaimed, "Whatever is the matter?"
>
> "Rose," he said, "you could never guess what he came for. He came as a deputation from the other evangelists and workers, yes, and servants, too, to ask what is the secret of the change in you. Before you went home, none of the servants wanted to serve you, but now they all want to be your servants."[6]

The "secret of the change in you"—this is the secret all with a longing soul yearn to know.

Thankfully, the secret is out! It all revolves around Christ in the believer and the believer in Christ—in short, the Christ Life, the revived life. Jesus Christ is the answer to the question, "*Who* shall deliver me?" The purpose of this book is to help readers experience Christ's life more abundantly by exploring the provision and accessibility of Christ's life. To do so we will first focus on three provisional truths. Then we will consider the key turning point in accessing that provision. Next we will address the day-by-day, moment-by-moment access of Christ's victorious life for both personal holiness and effective service.

After exploring the details of our blessed provision in Christ and our simple access to that provision by faith, we will step back to see how this whole package fits together from a scriptural standpoint.

Jesus said, "If any man thirst . . ." (John 7:37). Do you thirst? Jesus said, "Blessed are they which do hunger and thirst after righteousness: for they shall be filled" (Matt. 5:6). Is this the longing of your soul? Do you echo the cry of Paul, "O wretched man that I am! who shall deliver me from the body of this death?" (Rom. 7:24).

The answer is, "I thank God *through Jesus Christ* our Lord" (Rom. 7:25). Jesus lovingly said, "*I* am come that they might have life, and that they might have it more abundantly" (John 10:10).

The answer is Jesus—*the Christ Life Himself*—in all His abundance!

May we cry out with the psalmist, "O God, thou art my God; early will I seek thee: my soul thirsteth for thee, my flesh longeth for thee in a dry and thirsty land, where no water is; to see thy power and thy glory" (Psalm 63:1–2). The promise is sure, "For he satisfieth the *longing* soul, and filleth the *hungry* soul with goodness" (Psalm 107:9). You may join the ranks of those who have *sought* Jesus and *found* Him to be the delight of their souls.

If you have a longing soul, you have begun the adventure to freedom. The next chapter points you to the first necessary provision.

• • • • •

Questions for Personal Reflection

1. In what ways can you relate to the longing to be like Jesus?

2. What similarities or differences do you have with the examples of longing for victory represented by Hudson Taylor and Rosalind Goforth?

3. What hopes do you desire the Lord to fulfill through reading this book?

2

THE CLEAN HEART

The Provision of the Cleansing Power of the Blood

But if we walk in the light, as he is in the light, we have fellowship one with another, and the blood of Jesus Christ his son cleanseth us from all sin. . . . If we confess our sins, he is faithful and just to forgive us our sins, and to cleanse us from all unrighteousness. 1 John 1:7, 9

IN the early twentieth century, a young Christian man named John George Govan attended church in Scotland. He looked like a fine Christian man, but actually he pursued his own selfish ambitions. These ambitions were not intrinsically evil; they simply were not God's will for his life.

Then, in God's goodness, he heard some preaching on the subject of consecration. As he listened, he realized he was not consecrated. Later he wrote in his journal that he tried to consecrate himself on several occasions, but it didn't work. Notice *he tried to consecrate himself*—no wonder it didn't work! Many try to do this and end up frustrated at the lack of change.

In the providence of God, he heard a sermon on a clean heart and a filled life. The realization dawned upon him that he could not cleanse his own heart; he needed the Lord Jesus to do

19

a cleansing work in him. He also realized that in order for this cleansing work to take place, he must yield to the Spirit's work of conviction. He would have to surrender anything the Spirit of God indicated had to be given up—including his life's dreams. This he felt he could not do.

At that time his brother led in some special meetings at a nearby church. So John George Govan attended. That night the message addressed a clean heart. Again the Spirit brought conviction. But again he resisted the Holy Spirit. The next day he was miserable. However, he attended the evening meeting. This time, unlike his normal practice, he sat as far away from the pulpit as possible. Many, with radiant faces, testified to the power of a cleansed conscience. The Spirit bore witness with his spirit that the blessing to which they testified could have been his, if he had but yielded.

The preacher spoke and invited others to yield. Tragically, Govan resisted again. Then his brother, who led the meeting, noticed him in the back of the audience. Not knowing the spiritual turmoil he experienced at that moment, his brother called on him to close the service in prayer. Govan decided he would not attempt to just go through the motions. He knew he must decide which way he would take—the way of God's will or his own. So he stepped out into the aisle and paused to think it over. The whole audience waited. Then he got down on one knee, and with the entire congregation listening, he came clean with God. He surrendered his will and therefore surrendered all to God.

After the last "Amen," he stepped outside the church building into the cold Scottish air and commented to a friend, "I have a clean heart, I have trusted the Lord, and I know He has done it, though I don't feel any different." This claim revealed faith regardless of feeling. Later he wrote, "When I got home that night and went down before the Lord, then I knew the difference. The glory of God flooded my soul, and it has been different ever since."[7]

This difference soon led to an understanding of the "filled life." Later in God's leading, John George Govan founded the Faith Mission of Edinburgh, Scotland. Through this organization God used Govan to train young people in revival work, and many villages and towns were set aflame with revival fire as a result. In fact, it was Govan that God used to fan the flame of revival in the heart of a young man named Duncan Campbell who had come to the Faith Mission. Campbell saw the Lord bless in many revivals, including the Lewis Awakening of 1949–53. God used the watershed moment in Govan's life regarding a clean heart to bring much blessing to many others. Is there a need for this in your life?

The text states, "and the blood of Jesus Christ his Son cleanseth us from all sin." The blood is the provision for cleansing. Without question this is true for the legal cleansing of salvation. Hebrews 9:22 explains, "without shedding of blood is no redemption." Ephesians 1:7 affirms, "In whom [Jesus Christ] we have redemption through his blood, the forgiveness of sins."

But the blood is also the provision for the practical cleansing of sanctification. In fact, the writer John used the personal pronouns *we, us* and *our* throughout the first chapter of his epistle, indicating he had a cleansing for believers in mind. The blood of Jesus is the provision for both the legal cleansing in salvation, which affects our standing before God, and the practical cleansing in sanctification, which affects our walking with God. There must also be a cleansing beyond salvation.

Jesus illustrated this distinction when He washed the disciples' feet as recorded in John 13. When Peter protested, Jesus responded by saying, "If I wash thee not, thou hast no part with me." Then Peter reacted by saying, "Lord, not my feet only, but also my hands and my head." It was then that Jesus clarified the point of the illustration: "He that is washed [past tense] needeth not save to wash [present tense] his feet, but is clean every whit." In other words, the phrase "he that is washed" represents the full-body bath of salvation. However, as someone walks across the town of this world, his feet may pick up the dirt and defilement of the way. The phrase "needeth not save to wash his feet" represents the foot washing of sanctification. The former represents the legal cleansing, and the latter represents the practical cleansing.

Theologically speaking, Romans 4:7–8 explains this: "Blessed are they whose iniquities are forgiven, and whose sins are covered. Blessed is the man to whom the Lord will not impute sin." The moment you trusted Christ as your Savior, your past sins were forgiven, and your future sins will not be charged to your account. All of your sins—past, present and future—are "covered" by the blood of Jesus. But even though your future sins will not be charged to your account, and in that sense you are legally "safe," your future sins do break your fellowship with your heavenly Father and therefore need forgiveness and cleansing. First John 1 explains this specific provision.

Do you have a clean heart? Do you know it?

The blood is the provision for a clean heart, and you must avail yourself of Christ's provision. But how? First John 1:7 explains what to do, and verse 9 explains how to do it.

What to Do: Walk in the Light

First John 1:7 begins with a condition: "But if we walk in the light, as he is in the light . . ." The conditional "if" reveals that this involves human responsibility. It is not automatic. The condition is "if we walk in the light." This statement does not yet explain how to do this, but it does inform us as to what to do.

The standard for this condition is amazing: "walk in the light, *as he is in the light*." Whatever this is, it is a high standard. God dwells in the absolute light of His holiness where the seraphim ring out the anthem day and night, "Holy, holy, holy is the Lord God Almighty." And we are to "walk in the light, as he is in the light." How are we to do this?

Before answering that question, let's pause to consider the promise connected with the condition, "we have fellowship one with another." Who is the "one" and who is the "another"? The context provides the answer. Beginning two verses earlier, it states, "God is light, and in him [God] is no darkness at all. If we say that we have fellowship with him [God], and walk in darkness, we lie, and do not the truth: But if we walk in the light, as he [God] is in the light, we have fellowship one with another." The flow of the context indicates that the "one with another" is the believer and God. The emphasis is "vertical." According to verse three, there are "horizontal" ramifications. When we are in fellowship with God, we can be in fellowship with other believers who are also in fellowship with God. In fact, according to the next chapter, it is impossible to be in fellowship with God and hate your brother. But the emphasis of First John 1:7 is vertical.

When you walk in the light as God is in the light, you are restored to fellowship with that holy God, who dwells in the absolute light of His holiness. This is a stunning promise. Even while we still live in a sin-cursed body, the blood of Jesus can be so applied that we are restored to fellowship with our holy God this side of heaven! Truly there is power in the blood! "The blood of Jesus Christ his Son cleanseth us from all sin."

But how do you walk in the light, especially as He is in the light?

How to Do It: Confession and Faith

What are the steps on the pathway of walking in the light? First John 1:9 reveals two steps. The verse begins with a condition, "If we confess our sins," then follows with a promise, "he is faithful and just to forgive our sins, and to cleanse us from all unrighteousness." The first step is confession, based on the condition. The second step is faith, based on the promise.

Confession

The word "confess" literally means "to say the same thing." In the context it means to say the same thing that God—our holy God in heaven—says about our sin. This is walking in the light as He is in the light.

To say the same thing God says about sin involves at least three issues.

1. Call it sin.

Call it sin *accurately*. The corpse of sin must not be put in a beautiful coffin to make it seem not so bad. People often want to beautify the "deathliness" of sin by calling it a mistake, a disease or a syndrome, but they do not want to call it sin. However, confession means we must say the same thing God says about our sin.

Yet this leaves us in a dilemma because Jeremiah 17:9 states, "The heart is deceitful above all things, and desperately wicked: who can know it?" With such a deceitful heart, how can we "call it sin" accurately? Thankfully, Jeremiah 17:10 answers with, "I the LORD search the heart." We may ask God to give us a glimpse of what He sees in our hearts, so that we can say what He says. If you sincerely do this, God will give you that glimpse, and you will not like what you see. In fact, you will be mortified. But then you can say what God says about your sin.

Call it sin *thoroughly*. One of the several reasons for spiritual dullness is partial confession. A teen, who had been rebellious, responded to God's working during a real season of refreshing from the presence of the Lord at his church. He even went on to a Bible college to prepare for the ministry. A couple years later he mentioned to his pastor that he felt spiritually dull and wondered as to why this was the case. While acknowledging this young man had been turned around during the revival, the pastor suggested that perhaps he had never really recognized the wickedness of his teenage rebellion. The pastor then encouraged him to get alone with God and ask God to show him how wicked his rebellion really was. This would open his eyes so that he might deal thoroughly with his sin. Over a cup of coffee, this young man told me he followed his pastor's advice. Then he said, "Oh, what a day! I've never been the same since." God restored spiritual vitality through thorough confession.

Call it sin *without excuse*. We are masters at excusing our sin. We say things like, "Lord, I shouldn't have responded that way to so-and-so, but Lord, You know he provoked me." One man who had been confronted by his pastor regarding some severe marriage problems agreed he had blown it, but then said, "But let me tell you why I did it"—and blamed his wife. No wonder he had marriage problems!

Our flesh does not like the light. Even if we "confess," we often seek to excuse our sin, to justify it, to cover it up by blaming others or even the situation. All of this is an attempt to get out of the light. Ironically, this is walking in darkness in the name of walking in the light.

We do not like to think we are so bad. We con ourselves by thinking, "It's not really my fault. I would have never said that or done that. It was the situation. It was that other person; he just drew it out of me." However, in reality, "he" simply exposed what was already in you. Confession is getting honest and saying, "Regardless of anyone or anything else, I made sinful choices."

For example, some years ago I got in a "tiff" with another preacher. It was a carnal exchange at least on my part. As I walked away from it, the Holy Spirit was all over me with conviction. My first response was, "Well, he started it." In retrospect, I would suspect he thought I started it. But there was my attempt to shift blame.

The Holy Spirit would not let me off and continued to convict me. After several days and several states away in my travels, I decided to write a letter of apology. Today I am ashamed of this letter. It went something like this: "Dear Brother So-and-So: Because you did such-and-such, I did such-and-such. I should not have done that. Please forgive me," and so forth.

It should not be surprising that when I mailed the letter, I got no relief. Over the next period of weeks and months, the Lord kept convicting me. I remember arguing with the Lord, "Lord, I wrote a letter of apology, and Lord, it was a long letter." It had to be by the way I had written it.

Finally, I cried out, "Lord what is wrong?" Then the still small voice replied, "You're arrogant. Here you were supposedly writing a letter of apology, and all you did was to blame him." It was then I caught a glimpse into my own heart, and I did not like what I saw. In fact, I was mortified at what I had done. So I said, "What do You, Lord, want me to do?" The next letter was much shorter, and when I mailed it off, the burden rolled away and has never come back. Also, the Lord brought about reconciliation with that brother.

2. Give it up.

Proverbs 28:13 declares, "He that covereth his sins shall not prosper: but whoso confesseth and forsaketh them shall have mercy." Inherent in true confession is the necessity of forsaking the sin or simply giving up the sin. To go through the motions of confession while hanging on to the sin would be contradictory.

Confession is not merely confessing your guilt but confessing your sin. Many do not like the way they feel when they sin. They do not like the guilt. But quite frankly they still want their sin. Sadly, there is no sense of truly desiring a clean break with sin. Therefore, when they go through the motions of confession, they do not ever move on to victory.

How many men confess impure thoughts only to indulge their flesh at the next opportunity? When temptation arises, they do not look to God for deliverance. In fact, when temptation offers itself, at that point they do not even want deliverance. The reason is they have not given up the sin. They may have confessed their guilt, but they have not truly confessed their sin.

Some confess their sin even with emotion but then think, "Well, I'm sure I'll do it again." Or "If the circumstances are conducive, I'm sure I'll blow it." Undoubtedly they will, because they gave the ground by not giving up their sin. This is a form of nonsurrender. True confession says, "God, I give up this sin. I do not hold the right to ever take it again. But Lord, You know this is beyond me. I need supernatural deliverance." This is true surrender, which is true dependence upon God. This is the heart that, in the face of temptation, looks to the Deliverer and accesses His deliverance.

A man once told me that, although he had been a believer, he had a bad habit of cursing. He said he prayed for God to deliver him, but no deliverance came. Then a Christian brother told him God would not play tug-of-war with him—God would not deliver him while he was still hanging on to his end of the rope. He challenged him to let go of his end of the rope and then ask God for deliverance.

"The lights went on," my friend said. He told the Lord he was giving up the cursing, and there would be no more tug-of-war. Then he asked the Lord to deliver him. With a smile he testified to me that God then delivered him from the habit of cursing.

Just as waving the white flag of surrender involves giving up, so true confession involves giving up the issue. Some only mouth words of confession or even words that ask for deliverance (while still hanging on to the sin). But God says, call it sin, and *give it up*.

3. Make it right.

True confession also implies the readiness to make matters right. Generally speaking, the tenor of Scripture indicates that private sin demands private confession, personal sin (sinning against another person) demands personal confession, and public sin demands public confession. James 5:16 says, "Confess your faults one to another." The implication is that you have sinned against someone, and they know it (which will usually be obvious), or they have a right to know it.

Jesus said in the Sermon on the Mount in Matthew 5:23–24, "Therefore if thou bring thy gift to the altar, and there rememberest that thy brother hath ought against thee; leave there thy gift before the altar, and go thy way; first be reconciled to thy brother, and then come and offer thy gift." When a brother has "ought" or something against you, it implies you said or did something offensive. Jesus said essentially, "Go make it right." Then you can come and offer your gift.

Many desire the Spirit-filled life. For its fullest reality, this demands the presentation of one's all to be a living sacrifice as Romans 12:1 urges. This "gift," however, must be left at the altar until you are first reconciled with those who have something against you. You will short-circuit personal revival if you have those with whom you need to reconcile, and you disobey on this point. In fact, one of the greatest hindrances to revival is an unwillingness to humbly walk in the light in this fashion—especially if the other person "started it." But Jesus said, "Go make it right."

Is there anyone who has something against you because you sinned against them? In one of my local church meetings, a teenage girl responded during the invitation after I had addressed this truth. She sobbed her heart out to God. She had some tension with an unsaved girl at her public school. God convicted her of this, and the next day she went to the girl and apologized. Then she invited her to attend the service that night.

This unsaved girl, undoubtedly moved by this teen's humility, came to the service. The church girl led them to sit on the front row along with another unsaved teen she brought. God blessed, and both of the unsaved teens accepted Christ as their Savior. As the service dismissed and this young lady wiped tears from her eyes, I asked her if she had really done business with the Lord the night before. She acknowledged she had. I said, "You have just experienced a clean heart and a filled life, and God used you."

A lady from another meeting came to me on a Friday night and said, "I've apologized to three people." Then with an earnest face she said, "I have one more to go, and I'm going to have a clean heart." She followed through, and several years later when I returned, it was apparent she was well down the revival road.

These stories include "making it right" on the personal level. But the same principle is true on the public level. Several times I have seen people respond during an invitation and, after speaking to their pastor, have made matters right publicly. This has always been moving—sometimes dramatically so.

On one occasion a young Christian school teacher admitted to the congregation she had spoken evil to many of them of the other school teachers. Amid the sobs she asked for their forgiveness. Later that week she came by my book table with a gloriously radiant face. She had a clean heart.

In another meeting a lady came under conviction because she and another church lady had not spoken to each other for six years. The animosity toward each other was apparent to the church. So after getting right with the lady during the day, she publicly got right with the church that night. It was a powerful moment to eyewitness.

In summary, the first step on the pathway of walking in the light is confession. This step involves calling it sin, giving it up and making it right to the extent that it is appropriate. But there is another vital step to having a clean heart—and knowing it.

Faith

First John 1:9 does not stop with confession. The condition is followed by a promise: "he is faithful [every time] and just [because legally all your sins are covered by the blood] to forgive us our sins, and to cleanse us from all unrighteousness." This promise is the foundation of faith for a clean heart.

Understanding the Promise

The promise is threefold. First, God *releases* your debt. The word "forgive" means so much and includes the idea that God releases your sin debt and sends it away. For example, suppose someone borrowed a certain amount of money from you. That person would then owe you that amount of money. But suppose you decided to forgive the debt. You would be releasing the amount involved. Similarly, when you come clean with God,

He releases your sins and your guilt. What an amazing promise! Without this provision we would be forever in debt.

Second, God *removes* your sin. The phrase "cleanse us from all unrighteousness" is a glorious promise. The word "cleanse" conveys the idea of washing or purging. This implies God removes the "dirt" of sin. Although there are some sins which may have continuing ramifications, the sin itself can be cleansed. For example, when my father ministered in the Chicago area, he illustrated this truth by noting that if you got into a street fight and someone cut off your arm, you could be forgiven, but you would not get your arm back.

However, the glory of the promise is that the blood of Jesus does cleanse you from all your sin. The blood applied clears your conscience. What matters here is not how you may feel. What matters is that, from God's perspective, when you come clean with Him, the blood of Jesus cleans you up—completely.

Third, God *restores* your fellowship. Not only does God release the sin debt and remove the sin itself, He restores the contrite one to a place of fellowship (1 John 1:7).

Taking God at His Word

The promise is real. You must take a clean heart by faith. You must simply depend on the reality of God's promise and say, "I have a clean heart. I have trusted the Lord Jesus for it, and He has done it." Regardless of how you feel, just take God at His word.

The accuser of the brethren may suggest to you that this is too easy and you need to confess it all again. But if you confess the issue again without a new issue of stumbling, then you are listening to the wrong voice and stepping backward into unbelief. In one of my meetings where I had just dealt with this truth, a lady said to me, "I've done that for 50 years!" Then she sighed with relief at the thought of the promise and said, "Oh, what freedom!"

Some confess their sins, but then think they will have to wait several days or weeks before God will bless them again. But that is unbelief in God's immediate promise; it is also merit-based thinking. In reality, we do not ever merit blessing. Blessing comes only through the merit of Jesus. The fact is this: when you confess your sins, God releases, cleanses and restores so that you can trust Him to bless you right then and there—and He will.

Walking in the light is not sinless perfection; it is immediate confession. Immediate confession accesses immediate forgiveness. Consequently, the highway of holiness is the highway of lowliness. This is the heart that says, "Lord, if I stumble, please shine the light that I might walk in the light, that You might cleanse me and restore me and set me back up, that I might keep walking with You." Satan's lie is that since you stumbled, you might as well wallow in your sin. But this lie leads into "the slough of despond." God's truth is to walk in the light for cleansing and restoration.

Sinless Perfectionism

Occasionally, some charge those who explore the glorious truths of the Christ life with "sinless perfectionism." This is a gross misunderstanding because one of the great truths of the Christ life provision is the cleansing power of the blood. Interestingly, the verb "walk" in the phrase "walk in the light" in First John 1:7 and the verb "confess" in First John 1:9 are both in the present tense, emphasizing continuous action. The idea is "If we are walking in the light . . ." and "If we are confessing our sins . . . ." The use of the present tense implies you do not ever come to a point of sinless perfection where you no longer need to walk in the light by confessing your sins. While it is true the provision for victory over sin is perfect—Christ in you; it is not true we access that provision perfectly.

As Samuel Rutherford said in days gone by, "The closer you get to God, the less you sin. But the closer you get to God, the more you realize your sinfulness." The reason is that the closer you get to the light the more dirt you see that prior to that illumination you did not notice. In fact, when God began to bring me down the revival road, there was a period of time when God brought things to mind that I had not thought about for years. This light led to my being able to deal with those issues with both God and man. Soon the past was dealt with and settled.

It is a wonderful thing when, based on the promise of God, you know that you have a clean heart. If new issues arise and taint your heart, then you can immediately walk in the light of the Spirit's conviction and quickly know again the blessing of a clean heart.

Do you have a clean heart? Once at the end of a service where I had preached on this subject, a man came to me with tears in his eyes. As he shook my hand, he slowly and emphatically said, "I have a clean heart." Then he gripped my hand and exclaimed, "I have it!"

On another occasion a man testified that there were certain sins that had plagued him for years but now those sins were dealt with by the blood of Christ. As a tear rolled down his face, he said that, for the first time in a long time, he had a clean heart. The weight of his statement, spoken with such conviction, moved the audience.

At the end of another service, a lady stayed in her seat with her head resting on the chair in front of her. She sobbed quietly. After most of the church folk had left, she came out into the lobby where I was. A smile broke through a swollen face like a rainbow after the storm as she said, "I can finally say, *I have a clean heart!*"

Do you? What to do: walk in the light. How to do it: confession and faith. Whatever the Holy Spirit convicts you of, call
it sin, give it up and make it right. Then by faith take the clean
heart based on the sure promise of God. Once you have a clean
heart, the way is cleared for you to move on to the filled life.

• • • • •

Questions for Personal Reflection

1. What situations came to mind, if any, regarding confession
   without making excuses or seeking to shift blame?

2. What people came to mind, if any, regarding making matters right to the appropriate extent?

3. What issues came to mind, if any, regarding the need to take
   the step of faith for a clean heart?

3

THE EXCHANGED LIFE
The Provision of the Enabling Power of the Spirit

Christ, who is our life . . . COLOSSIANS 3:4

B Y thirty-seven years of age, Hudson Taylor had already
founded the China Inland Mission and had experienced a
measure of blessing. Yet he thirsted for greater personal victory. He would begin the day desiring victory over irritability
and impatience. But by the end of the day, he was confessing the
same sins he had confessed the day before. Although he knew
there was a greater victory available in Christ, he did not know
how to access that victory.

In this time of deep heart searching, Hudson Taylor received
a letter from a colleague in the mission named McCarthy, who
was on a similar pilgrimage and had been awakened to a life-
changing truth. We referenced this fact in the first chapter, but
we did not disclose the articulation of the life-changing truth. In
this letter of testimony, the Holy Spirit spoke to Hudson Taylor
through the following words: "Not a striving to have faith . . .
but a looking off to the Faithful One seems all we need." It was
as if the clouds parted and sunlight shone into his heart. He

knew faith was the victory, but he had been focusing on his having faith rather than on the object of faith—the Faithful One.

When Hudson Taylor looked at the object of faith, Jesus Christ, he saw an all-sufficient Savior—sufficient for every need, trial, temptation and circumstance. As he looked unto Jesus, the Spirit of Jesus authored faith in his heart, and he began to experience a transformation, especially in regard to irritability and impatience. So real was this personal revival, he spoke of it constantly in person and in letters to his friends and relatives. In his own words he said, "Oh, the joy of seeing this truth!"[8]

What happened to Hudson Taylor? He learned to regularly exchange his life for the life of Jesus Christ. This continual exchange is "the exchanged life." If you know Jesus Christ as your Savior, then factually, you have already exchanged your sin for the credited righteousness of Jesus Christ, and you have already exchanged the destiny of hell for the destiny of heaven, where you will exchange mortality for immortality and faith for sight. However, there is an exchanged life available now in between justification and glorification.

"Christ, who is our life . . ." Have you discovered the blessing of the exchanged life? Perhaps you may be wondering what exactly the exchanged life is all about. Colossians unfolds the provision for the exchanged life and the potential of the exchange.

Understanding the Provision

The provision of the exchanged life entails three major concepts discussed in Colossians 3.

1. The New Man

This first concept involves an exchange that takes place in the human spirit. Colossians 3:3 states, "For ye are dead [you died] and your life is hid with Christ in God." Since the Scripture affirms that as a believer "you died," it begs the question, "Which part of you died?" Physical death is the separation of the soul from the body. Obviously, physical death has not yet occurred for you. The death in Colossians 3:3 cannot, then, refer to your soul or body. Consequently, there is only one part of you left: your spirit.

Colossians 3:9 describes it this way: ". . . seeing that ye have put off the old man with his deeds." The verb tense of the words "have put off" indicates the fact of an action, and the defining sense literally means to take off completely. Whatever "ye have put off the old man" refers to, it has been done. It is not partial but complete. This parallels Romans 6:6: "Knowing this, that our old man is [was] crucified with him." Again, since your soul and body have not been crucified, the wording "old man" must refer to your human spirit. This observation is important.

Colossians 3:10 follows saying, "and have put on the new man." The verb tense again indicates the fact of an action. If you are a believer in Jesus Christ, then a part of you died. A separation took place; you have put off the old man. Yet through resurrection you have put on the new man. Literally, your old man has been exchanged for your new man. But what does all this mean?

Prior to salvation your old man (human spirit) was unregenerated. This simply means your human spirit was separated from the life of God or, as Ephesians 4:18 describes, "alienated from the life of God." Death essentially means separation. Therefore, prior to salvation you were separated from God. Ephesians 2:1 further explains "dead in trespasses and sins." You were dead to God, but you were alive to sin, as the phrase "dead in trespasses and sins" makes clear. Dead to God but alive to sin. Separated from God but joined to sin. In the immaterial part of your being, your old man (unregenerated spirit) was united with in-dwelling sin, or what Romans 7:17 and 20 describes as "sin that dwelleth in me." You were in a relationship with the master—the taskmaster—of indwelling sin.

This was an incredibly bad union from which only the sepa-ration of death could sever. How could this death take place? It could only take place through your identification with Christ and His death. Christ not only "died *for* our sins" (1 Cor. 15:3), He "died *unto* sin" (Rom. 6:10). To die unto sin, Jesus had to come into union with our sin. On the cross God the Son was separated from God the Father—because He was in union with our sin. This is utterly amazing. Since Jesus came to save sinners, I believe this was why Jesus agonized in the garden and why He later cried out, "My God, my God, why hast thou forsaken me?" He did not shrink back from His purpose to save sinners, but from the method of having to be separated from the Father and united with the sin of the world.

But "he died unto sin once" (Rom. 6:10). When you be-lieved on Jesus as your Savior, God identified you in Him and, therefore, in His history, including His death. So at the moment of saving faith, you died unto sin. Your old man was completely put off. Your union with indwelling sin was forever broken. You are no longer joined to the taskmaster of indwelling sin. Better still, you were raised with Christ a new man. The new man was put on, and therefore, your human spirit was regenerated. The old man was exchanged for the new man. The unregenerated spirit was exchanged for the regenerated spirit.

2. The New Union

Even better, your new man (regenerated spirit) is now in a new union with the eternal life of Jesus who "moved in" at sal-vation. When you believed on Jesus, you "received him" (John

1:12) who is "that eternal life" (1 John 1:2). The Spirit of Christ moved in and joined your regenerated spirit, and "he that is joined unto the Lord is one spirit" (1 Cor. 6:17). Now you are "dead indeed unto sin, but alive unto God through Jesus Christ our Lord" (Rom. 6:11). You are no longer dead to God and thus separated from God; you are no longer alive to indwelling sin and thus joined to indwelling sin. Instead, you are now dead to indwelling sin and thus separated from indwelling sin; you are alive to God and thus joined to the Holy Spirit. The old relationship with indwelling sin is forever severed, and the new relationship with the indwelling Christ is forever sealed. What a glorious exchange!

Although the former master of indwelling sin still seeks to operate within your body and usurp his former place of authority by urging you to bow to him, he is no longer your authority. You are no longer joined to him. Formerly your service to indwelling sin was forced labor. Now it can only be voluntary service. You have a New Master who is a good master, who will enable you to do whatever He bids.

Your old master of indwelling sin has been exchanged for the new master of the indwelling Christ. "Christ . . . our life" is simply the Spirit of Christ filling you with the life of Christ. This is often termed the Spirit-filled life or the Christ life. "Christ in you" (Col. 1:27), "Christ liveth in me" (Gal. 2:20), "For to me to live is Christ" (Phil. 1:21) all reveal that human animation can be exchanged for divine animation. Mere natural ability can be exchanged for supernatural ability. The lower life of "just you" can be exchanged for the higher life of "Christ in you."

Your best for Christ can be exchanged for His best in you. For your best for Christ is insufficient until it is Christ's best in you. This is not a matter of what you, on your own, do *for* Christ; it is a matter of what He does *through* you. Not Christ instead of you, but Christ through you as you cooperate, from inside the deepest part of your being, energizing and animating your personality with His divine victorious life. What a potential difference! Only then can what you do for Christ be truly *for* Christ.

While there is still a battle between the flesh (where indwelling sin still seeks to operate) and the Spirit (Gal. 5:17), and a choice between walking after the flesh or after the Spirit (Rom. 8:4), the contestants in this battle are not equals. You must spiritually grasp this reality.

The battle between flesh and Spirit has been likened to two dogs battling inside of you, and whichever one you feed and favor the most will win. But this illustration can be misleading. While it is true your choices do make a difference, do we not in our mind's eye picture two dogs of the same size? If that were the case, the contestants would be equals, and sometimes one dog would be dominant, and sometimes the other dog would. But the contestants in the battle between flesh and Spirit are not equals. Not even a little dog like a Chihuahua verses a large dog like a Rottweiler would provide an accurate picture!

Consider for a moment the contestant of the "Spirit." Some may wonder, "Are you referring to the regenerated human spirit or the Holy Spirit?" The answer is "Yes!" Remember "he that is joined to the Lord is one spirit" (1 Cor. 6:17). This is an amazing statement.

Let's consider both parties in the union. Your new man (regenerated spirit) is "a new creature" or creation (2 Cor. 5:17). This new creation is described as "the seed [*sperma*] of God" (1 John 3:9). Something of the nature of God has been implanted into you. This seed of God is "the new man, which after God is created in righteousness and true holiness" (Eph. 4:24). Your regenerated spirit, as the new man, is righteous and holy. It must be, for it is God's own nature implanted into you, and it must be, because it becomes the dwelling place of the *Holy* Spirit. The Holy Spirit unites with your regenerated human spirit. This union connects you to the enthroned Christ. For the indwelling Spirit is described as the Spirit of "him who is raised from the dead" (Rom. 7:4) and who now sits at the right hand of the Father on the throne far above the powers of darkness (Eph. 1:19–21).

The provision for victory is perfect. It has to be—His name is Jesus! Sadly, it is our access of Him that is imperfect. But the provision is perfect. When we access our union with the conquering, triumphant Christ, the Chihuahua of the flesh is no match!

Some say the Christian life is too hard. This shows a flesh-dependent perspective, and from that perspective the Christian life is not just hard, it is impossible. If you are thinking, "I can't forgive" or "I can't love" or "I can't be patient" and so forth, you are right. But Jesus can! This is not a matter of Christ helping you to live *your* life. It is a matter of Christ living *His* very life through your personality. Christ is our life.

The Christian life is not merely a set of doctrines. It is not merely a set of moral actions. Unsaved moralists can mimic that. Rather, the Christian life is a *life*, a Person, and His name is Jesus. Jesus Christ is *the Christian Life*. Therefore, no one can live the Christian life, but Christ. But the good news is that when you were born again, Christ, *the Christian Life*, moved in to impart to you that *Life* so that you can live—yet not you but Christ in you—the Christian life. When you experience Christ's life, you experience *the Christ life*. This is not a matter of imitation, but impartation. True Christlikeness accesses Christ's life as the animation to your personality. This is truly the revived life.

Do You Still Have an Old Nature?

The word "nature" (*phusis*) is used fourteen times in the New Testament with several potential meanings, including natural condition, natural order or laws, natural being, physical origin, habit and natural characteristics. In some cases lexicons vary as to what definitions apply to particular passages. The terminology *old nature* and *new nature* is not found in New Testament usage as such. The closest possibility would be perhaps "partakers of the divine nature" (2 Pet. 1:4). Rather the New Testament speaks of three contrasts: the "old man" and the "new man," indwelling sin (e.g. "sin that dwelleth in me," "the law of sin," etc.) and the indwelling Christ (e.g. "Christ in you," "Christ liveth in me," etc.), and "flesh" and "spirit" or "Spirit." So does a believer still have an old nature?

Theologians seem to have varying "spins" on the answer to this question, making it largely a matter of semantics. If you are speaking of indwelling sin or the flesh, then yes, unquestionably,

3. The New Victory

The first major concept addressed exchanging the old man (unregenerated spirit) for the new man (regenerated spirit). The second major concept addressed exchanging the master of indwelling sin for the master of the indwelling Christ. The two concepts combined explain the new union of the new man with the new life: "Christ who is our life." For every believer these two major concepts represent facts that have already occurred. These facts, sometimes called "positional truth," provide the foundation for function or "practical truth." Now there can be an exchange of habits. Based on the new position, there can be a transformed practice.

Colossians 3:4 explains, "When Christ, who is our life shall appear [be manifested], then shall ye also appear [be manifested] with him in glory." This will be ultimately demonstrated when our bodies are glorified, but in the spiritual realm this can be demonstrated now. When Christ is allowed to be manifested through you, His glory is seen. The passage continues, "Mortify therefore" (3:5) and refers back to the provision of "Christ . . . our life." Only by trusting Christ as our life can the command to mortify be obeyed. The word "mortify" means "put to death." Since the old man has been put to death (because he was taken off completely when he died with Christ) it is the habits of the old man that need to be put to death. "Mortify therefore your members which are upon the earth; fornication [sexual sin of any kind], uncleanness [all the compromises that lead to sexual sin], inordinate affection [passion], evil concupiscence [evil desire], and covetousness, which is idolatry" (3:5). Remember you still have an old nature. But if you are speaking strictly of the old man, then no, you do not have an old nature, because the old man died with Christ and was raised the new man, and you cannot have an unregenerated spirit and a regenerated spirit in the same body. The old man is gone—forever. But you still have your former master of indwelling sin who seeks to operate within your flesh.

It seems best to include all the biblical terminologies in the concept of the old nature. This means that prior to salvation your old nature was comprised of the union between your *old man* (unregenerated spirit) and *indwelling sin*, both of which operated within your *flesh*. At salvation this union was severed as you (your human spirit) died with Christ unto indwelling sin and were raised with Christ to join Him as the indwelling Christ. Therefore, now your old nature consists only of your former master of *indwelling sin* who still seeks to operate within your *flesh*.

that Paul, under inspiration, just stated to the Colossian saints that Christ was their life. Paul was and is writing to believers. Yet evidently they had some real "baggage" that needed to be exchanged. "For which things' sake the wrath of God cometh on the children of disobedience" (3:6) emphasizes that the un-regenerated will be judged eternally for this. "In the which ye also walked some time, when ye lived in them" (3:7). In other words, "You're saved now, so let's deal with the former bad habits by the power of Christ who is our life."

In a local church meeting, I was told of one in the church who used to be a homosexual. But he had believed in Jesus, and through Jesus as his new life, he "put to death" this old sinful habit. Christ is sufficient to deal with any sin of the flesh!

The text in Colossians 3 moves beyond outer-man sins to inner-man sins. "But now ye also put off all these; anger, wrath [blowing up], malice [clamming up], blasphemy, filthy commu-nication out of your mouth. Lie not one to another, seeing that ye have put off the old man with his deeds." Since you have put off the old man with all that he was, now put off all that he was about. In other words, since you have put off the old man, now put off the habits of the old man.

Positively the next verse says,

> *And have put on the new man. . . .* Put on therefore [based on this new union] . . . mercies, kindness, humbleness of mind, meekness, longsuffering; forbearing one another, and forgiv-ing one another, if any man have a quarrel against any: even as Christ forgave you, so also do ye. And above all these things put on charity [love], which is the bond of perfectness. (3:10, 12–14)

In other words, since you have put on the new man, now put on the habits of the new man.

Through the power of Christ as one's very life, the works

of the flesh can be exchanged for the fruit of the Spirit, old ways can be exchanged for new ways, and bad habits can be exchanged for good habits. Truly there is hope! The former bad habits you acquired before you were saved, and even after you were saved, by yielding to your flesh can be exchanged for new, good, acquired habits. Instead of being regularly defeated and surprised by victory, you can be regularly victorious and surprised by defeat!

Rosalind Goforth, whom we also referenced in the first chapter, experienced this transformation. Although she had a bad habit of impatience and irritability, she found that when she exchanged her life for Christ's life, He was patient without irritation. Over time, as she kept making this exchange, she developed a new habit of patience. Others, with other issues, discover that when they exchange their lives for Christ's life, He does not worry, He does not overeat, He is punctual, and so forth. The life of Christ is transformational yet practical.

Whether speaking of the evil works of unrighteousness or the dead works of self-righteousness, all can be exchanged for the good works of Christ's righteousness. A good work is not a good work unless it is energized by the only one that is good, and that is God (Matt. 19:17). But how can the new man access the new union to enable new victory? How do you make the exchange? What is our part, and what is God's part? At this point we will only briefly address our responsibility in making the exchange, since we will develop this more fully in chapter five. But we will take time to address the potential of "God's part."

Understanding the Potential

The Holy Spirit uses the truth of the provision for the exchanged life to stir us to respond. When we do respond rightly, He supernaturally enables us. What is our responsibility?

Man's Responsibility

Colossians 2:6 explains, "As ye have therefore received Christ Jesus the Lord, so walk ye in him." This verse explains both *what* to do and *how* to do it.

What to Do

The "what" of man's responsibility is to "walk ye in him." Galatians 5:16 states it this way: "Walk in the Spirit, and ye shall not fulfill the lusts of the flesh." Both verses are imperative and in the present tense. The command is not referring to a once-for-all event but to a continuous responsibility. Even the word "walk" indicates repeated steps. In this sense "the exchanged life" is a life that regularly exchanges the self-life for the Christ life.

When this exchange is made, "ye shall not fulfill the lusts of the flesh." As a college student, this promise thrilled me. But then I wondered, "What does it mean to walk in the Spirit?"

How to Do It

What is walking but reiterated steps? Therefore, walking in the Spirit is simply reiterated steps in the Spirit. Reiterated steps obviously are made one step at a time. You need not focus on the past or fear the future. A present step of walking in the Spirit accesses a present enabling by the Spirit. But what is a "step in the Spirit"? How do you do that?

Colossians 2:6 explains, "*As ye have therefore received* Christ Jesus the Lord, *so walk ye* in him." How do you walk in the Spirit or walk in Him? The same way you received Christ—through the surrender of faith. You simply surrendered to the conviction of the Holy Spirit about sin, righteousness and judgment, trusting in Christ as your Savior. In the same way, surrender to the workings of the Holy Spirit in simple faith, trusting Him for the step at hand.

Man's responsibility is simply the surrender of faith, regarding both the leadership of the Spirit and the enabling by the Spirit. This is the "so walk ye in him." It is a simple trust in God's purpose and power. It is the opposite of depending on the flesh or walking "after the flesh" (Rom. 8:4). Depending on the flesh is not only self-indulgence in the "works of the flesh" (Gal. 5:19) but also self-dependence in the strength of the flesh, described as "the man that trusteth in man, and maketh flesh his arm, and whose heart departeth from [trusting in] the LORD" (Jer. 17:5). It is possible to try to live the Christian life without depending on *the Christian Life* Himself—Christ.

This kind of dependence on the flesh manifests itself in three primary ways revolving around the soul of man: mind, affections and will. First, there is *intellectual* dependence, where the primary focus is on mere logic, and the self-proclaimed thought is, "We're the intellects in theology." Second, there is *emotional* dependence, where the primary focus is on mere experience, and the self-proclaimed thought is, "You haven't arrived until you've experienced what we've experienced." Third, there is *volitional* dependence, where the primary focus is on sheer willpower, and the self-proclaimed thought is, "*We* can do it!" Ironically, those who are of one bent often look down upon those who are of the other two, when in reality each one is no higher than the other because they are all on the soul level.

In the exchanged life all dependence on the flesh must be exchanged for dependence on God. Walking in the sphere of the flesh must be exchanged for walking in the sphere of the Spirit. While the soul of man is most definitely involved in walking in the Spirit, yet since walking in the Spirit is walking by faith, the dependence is clearly on God. The mind understands the scriptural provision of the new man and the new union to enable a new living. The affections are "affected" by this understanding, being convinced of its reality. And then the will is exercised by depending on the indwelling Christ for the Christ life. This is not the soul depending on itself; it is the soul cooperating in depending on God.

But to "walk" in Him demands taking steps, and a step demands not only believing God can do something but depending on Him to do it. This completes the picture of surrender/faith choices for divine leadership and enabling. It is *trusting to obey*. For example, the story is told of a man who once asked Andrew Murray to pray for him so that he would get up in the morning to read his Bible and pray. Andrew Murray responded by saying that if the man would put his first leg out of bed he would pray for God to enable him to get the second leg out! This incisive comment exposes a common deception. Many are seeking a "divine zap." But God waits for us to take the given step of faith, at which time He enables us to follow through.

God's Promise

Colossians 3 teaches that when you depend on Christ as your life, you can replace bad habits with good habits by His divine enabling. This is the principle of counteraction, where a greater law overcomes a lesser law.

Consider a room that has been wired with electricity and connected to a power source. Without light the room is filled with darkness. You might say that there is a tendency to darkness or that the law of darkness prevails. But with the single flip of a switch, the electrical power is accessed, and the law of light counteracts the law of darkness. However, if the switch is turned off, then the law of darkness returns. But as long as the switch is on the "on" position, the light overcomes the darkness.

When you got saved, you got wired! You are connected to the inexhaustible power source of *Christ in you*. Without Him you will fail because there is a tendency to sin or a law of sin that prevails. But with the simple flip of a switch—the surrender of faith—you access Christ's life, and the law of the Spirit counteracts the law of sin. However, if you say no to the Spirit on a particular matter, the law of sin takes back over. But as long as you keep saying yes to the Holy Spirit, then the indwelling Christ keeps overcoming indwelling sin.

Consider an extension cord. By itself it is useless. But if on one end you plug the extension cord into a power outlet and on the other end you plug an appliance into it, though the cord itself does not become powerful, it does become a conduit of power.

Similarly, you are like an extension cord. By yourself—not "plugged in" to Christ as your life and not taking any steps of obedience—you are useless. Jesus said, "Without me ye can do nothing" (John 15:5). But if on the one hand you "plug in" to Christ as your life and on the other hand you take a step of faith, though you do not become powerful, you do become a channel of power.

Now suppose you plug an appliance into an extension cord, but you do not plug the other end into a power outlet, what would happen? Nothing would. This pictures you when you try to obey without trusting Christ in you to enable you to obey. This can only produce the form of godliness that denies the power thereof (2 Tim. 3:5).

Suppose you plug the extension cord into the power outlet, but you do not plug any appliance into the other end, what would happen? Nothing would. This imagery pictures you when you say you trust God, but you never take a step of faith. This would be "easy-believism" on sanctification or service.

The answer is not "Just obey" (depending on the flesh) or "Just trust" (easy-believism). The answer is "Trust to obey" (depending on God for Spirit-enabled obedience). This is the exchanged life. It is the Spirit-filled life. It is the Spirit filling you with the life of Jesus Christ.

Making the exchange allows you to be a practical partaker of the divine nature (2 Pet. 1:3–4). Making this exchange on a daily basis allows you to lose your life and yet save it by accessing Christ as your life. When you save your life through self-will (leadership) and self-dependence (enabling), you veil Christ's life and lose yours. Such a life of depending on the flesh will be exposed as wood, hay and stubble, and incinerated in the judgment seat fires (1 Cor. 3). This is a great loss of your life—what your life was wrapped up in. You will be saved, yet so as by fire, and any rewards will be forfeited.

But when you lose your life through depending on God's will (leadership) and God's strength (enabling), you unveil Christ's life and find your life now energized and animated by His. You truly find that your life can be all God intended it to be through the exchanged life. The life of dependence on God will be manifested as gold, silver and precious stones at the judgment seat fires. God—Christ in you and through you—meets the standard of God. Rewards will be given. Since faith is not a work but dependence upon the Worker, you will be rewarded for what Christ in you earned—amazing.

My father demonstrated the exchanged life. A missionary told me he once spent two hours with my father at an airport. Although he did not know my father well, he said God used those two hours to change his life. How could this be? Simply because the powerful dynamic was not merely the life of my father; it was the life of Jesus Christ manifested through a weak but surrendered and dependent channel.

Have you discovered the blessing of the exchanged life? A clean heart may become a filled life whereby the emptiness of the self-life is exchanged regularly for the fullness of the Christ life. However, when you enter the Spirit-filled life in earnest, you enter into a spiritual realm with a whole new set of dynamics. You are now ready to discover your provision in Christ for spiritual warfare.

· · · · ·

Questions for Personal Reflection

1. How was your thinking challenged regarding being "dead to sin"?

2. How was your faith built regarding your new relationship with the indwelling Christ?

3. What other examples of the "principle of counteraction" can you think of?

4

THE THRONE SEAT

The Provision of the Authoritative Power of the Throne

Blessed be the God and Father of our Lord Jesus Christ, who hath blessed us with all spiritual blessings in heavenly places in Christ. EPHESIANS 1:3

And what is the exceeding greatness of his power to us-ward who believe, according to the working of his mighty power, which he wrought in Christ, when he raised him from the dead, and set him at his own right hand in the heavenly places, far above all principality, and power, and might, and dominion, and every name that is named, not only in this world, but also in that which is to come: and hath put all things under his feet, and gave him to be the head over all things to the church, which is his body, the fullness of him that filleth all in all. EPHESIANS 1:19–23

And you hath he quickened, who were dead in trespasses and sins . . . and hath raised us up together, and made us sit together in heavenly places in Christ Jesus. EPHESIANS 2:1, 6

IN the midst of the Lewis Awakening, which took place from 1949–53 on the island of Lewis located off the northwest coast of Scotland, Duncan Campbell began holding services in the little town of Bernera. God used a young lad to intercede at a key moment.

The atmosphere was heavy and preaching difficult, so he [Campbell] sent to Barvas for some of the men to come and assist in prayer. They prayed, but the spiritual bondage persisted, so much so that halfway through his address Duncan stopped preaching. Just then he noticed this boy, visibly moved, under a deep burden for souls. He thought: "That boy is in touch with God and living nearer to the Savior than I am." So leaning over the pulpit he said, "Donald, will you lead us in prayer?"

The lad rose to his feet and in his prayer made reference to the fourth chapter of Revelation, which he had been reading that morning: "O God, I seem to be gazing through the open door. I see the Lamb in the midst of the Throne, with the keys of death and of hell. . . ." He began to sob; then lifting his eyes toward heaven, cried: "O God, there is power there; let it loose!" With the force of a hurricane the Spirit of God swept into the building and the floodgates of heaven opened. The church resembled a battlefield. . . . many were . . . weeping and sighing . . . . God had come.

The spiritual impact of this visitation was felt throughout the island; people hitherto indifferent were suddenly arrested and became deeply anxious. The contributor of an article to the local press, referring to the results of this movement, wrote: "More are attending the weekly prayer-meetings than attended public worship on the Sabbath before the revival."[9]

This is a beautiful example of a child of God accessing throne seat authority.

Jesus said, "At that day ye shall know that I am in my Father, and *ye in me*, and *I in you*" (John 14:20). The truth of *the believer in Christ* is just as invigorating as the truth of *Christ in the believer.* The "in Christ" phrases occur approximately thirty-five times in Ephesians, more than any other New Testament book. As the previous chapter, "The Exchanged Life," focuses on "Christ in you," so this chapter, "The Throne Seat," focuses on "you in Christ." To be "in Christ" is to be at the throne where Christ sits "far above all." This is the place of authority.

Building on the access of divine ability, believers may also exercise divine authority in the spiritual realm. Are you exercising the authority of your throne seat? What is the basis for this authority? The Scripture provides three realities you must comprehend as the basis for exercising throne seat authority.

1. Comprehend the Person of Authority

Jesus said, "All power [authority] is given unto me in heaven and in earth" (Matt. 28:18). Our text says, "He raised him from the dead, and set him at his own right hand in the heavenly places, far above all principality, and power, and might, and dominion, and every name that is named, not only in this world, but also in that which is to come" (Eph. 1:20–21). The key to spiritual warfare is to focus on the Victor—Christ, the conquering King. This involves comprehending the King and His kingdom.

The King

Christ is the King with all authority for the following reasons:

God delegated the kingdom of earth to Adam. Genesis 1:26 states, "And God said, Let us make man in our image, after our likeness: and let them have *dominion* over the fish of the sea, and over the fowl of the air, and over the cattle, and over all the earth, and over every creeping thing.." Adam and Eve had been given "dominion" or authority "over all the earth," specifically the "fish," "fowl," "cattle" and "every creeping thing." Therefore, when Satan came as a serpent, Adam and Eve had the authority to say, "In the name of the Lord, 'be gone!'"

Adam legally delivered the kingdom of earth to Satan. In obeying Satan's lie, Adam and Eve did not become "as gods" (literally, "like God") as Satan promised; they became Satan's slaves. For Romans 6:16 says, "His servants ye are to whom ye obey" and Second Peter 2:19 confirms, "Of whom a man is overcome, of the same is he brought again in bondage." When Adam became Satan's slave, Satan became the owner of all that Adam possessed—the kingdom of earth. At this time Satan became "the prince of this world" (John 12:31; 16:11) and "the god of this world" (2 Cor. 4:4).

In the temptation of Christ recorded in Luke 4:5–7, Satan "shewed unto him all *the kingdoms of the world.* . . . And the devil said unto him, All this power [authority] will I give thee, and the glory of them *for that is delivered unto me*; and to whomsoever I will I give it. If thou therefore wilt worship me, all shall be thine." In order to package an effective lie, there must be some misuse of truth. The truth that was being misused was the fact that the kingdom of earth had been legally "delivered" over to Satan.

As Satan sought to get the first Adam to obey him rather than God, he sought to get the second Adam to do likewise. But what Satan achieved with the first Adam, he failed to accomplish with the second Adam! However, since the kingdom of earth had been legally delivered over to Satan, it would have to be legally regained.

Christ legally regained the kingdom of earth. Sin had to be atoned for and the wages of sin paid in order for the authority of Satan to be broken. Genesis 3:15 prophesied, "And I will put enmity between thee [the serpent of Satan] and the woman, and between thy seed and her seed; it shall bruise thy head, and thou shalt bruise his heel." For us today this prophetical event is now in the past. At the cross Christ bruised the head of the serpent. Satan has been dealt a death blow. Although God allows him to squirm for a while to test the hearts of men, he has been defeated.

Just a few hours before the cross and referring to the power of the cross, Jesus said, "The prince of this world is judged"(John 16:11) and "Now is the judgment of this world: now shall the prince of this world be cast out"(John 12:31). Hebrews 2:14 affirms, "That through death he might destroy [render ineffective] him that had the power of death, that is, the devil." Colossians 2:14–15 further explains, "Blotting out the handwriting of ordinances that was against us, which was contrary to us, and took it out of the way, nailing it to his cross; And having spoiled [disarmed] principalities and powers, he made a shew [public spectacle] of them openly, triumphing over them in it."

Sin was atoned for! The wages of sin were paid! Jesus Christ, through the cross, legally regained the kingdom of earth, and therefore, He now has all authority as the reigning King![10]

The Kingdom

A king must of necessity have a kingdom, and a kingdom involves both subjects and a realm.

The Subjects: Regarding all believers in Jesus, Colossians 1:13 declares, "Who hath delivered us from the power [authority] of darkness, and hath translated us into the kingdom of his dear Son." Which kingdom are you in? The choice to actually depend on Jesus as your Savior from sin and hell not only accesses salvation; it is also the moment you are delivered from the authority of darkness and "translated" into a new realm of authority, which is the kingdom of Christ.

The Realm: Christ won all at the cross, but He is taking the kingdom He won in stages.

First, there is the *present kingdom*, which represents *a spiri-*

tual realm. Jesus said in Matthew 12:28, "But if I cast out devils by *the Spirit of God*, then *the kingdom of God* is come unto you." This indicates there is a present "kingdom" that relates to the work of "the Spirit of God." The present dominion is manifested in the spiritual realm, not the physical realm. However, where the spiritual realm interpenetrates the physical realm, there may be ramifications in the physical realm, as in the casting out of demons from physical bodies by the power of the Spirit.

Second, there is the *future kingdom*, which represents both *a spiritual and a physical realm.* This coming kingdom is described often in Isaiah and Revelation. However, what will be manifested in the physical realm is true now in the spiritual realm. This truth explains the reason why so many passages in Isaiah have been blessed to the hearts of those interceding for revival.

2. Comprehend the Position of Authority

Our text in Ephesians states:

And what is the exceeding greatness of his power to us-ward who believe, according to the working of his mighty power, which he wrought in Christ, when he raised him from the dead, and set him at his own right hand in the heavenly places, far above all principality, and power, and might, and dominion, and every name that is named, not only in this world, but also in that which is to come: and hath put all things under his feet, and gave him to be the head over all things to the church, which is his body, the fulness of him that filleth all in all. . . . And you hath he quickened, who were dead in trespasses and sins . . . and hath raised us up together, and made us sit together in heavenly places in Christ Jesus. (Eph. 1:19–23; 2:1, 6)

This amazing passage conveys two pertinent thoughts regarding the position of authority.

Christ's Position

The main emphasis regards Christ's position.

The Description of a Power Display: Ephesians 1:19 incorporates four "power words" to describe the display of God's power when He raised Christ from the dead and seated Him at His own right hand on the throne: "power" (*dunimis*), emphasizing ability; "working" (*energeia*), emphasizing energy; "mighty" (*kratos*), emphasizing sheer strength; "power" (*ischus*), emphasizing dominion. This is the only scriptural passage that incorporates four "power words" for something and, as such, indicates a very special significance.

The Events of the Power Display: When Ephesians 1:20 states, "Which he wrought in Christ, *when he raised him from the dead,* and *set him at his own right hand* in the heavenly places," it refers to two major events as the reasons for this power display: the resurrection and the enthronement of Christ. The resurrection of Christ's human body was the first human body to be raised into a glorified body, making Christ "the firstborn from the dead" (Col. 1:18). The enthronement of Christ was the sign of regained authority whereby "he is the head . . . that in all things he might have the preeminence" (Col. 1:18).

The Result of the Power Display: Ephesians 1:21–22 describes Christ's position at the throne as "far above all principality, and power [authority], and might, and dominion, and every name that is named, not only in this world, but also in that which is to come: and hath put all things under his feet." Jesus Christ sits in the position of authority "far above all . . . ." Jesus is the enthroned Christ!

The Believer's Position

In addition to Christ's position, we must comprehend the believer's position in Christ.

Co-resurrection and Co-enthronement: Ephesians 2:1 and 6 detail a remarkable continuation of thought: "*And you* hath he . . . raised . . . and made [to] sit together in heavenly places in Christ." This declaration reveals that when God raised Christ,

He raised us *in Christ*, and when God seated Christ at the throne, He seated us *in Christ* at the throne, for the Head and the body must of necessity be raised together and seated together (Eph. 1:22–23). God displayed His mighty power when He raised Christ *and you* and when He seated Christ *and you*. Everyone *in Christ* was a part of this power display.

The resurrection and the enthronement of Christ included both the Head and the body. "Christ, as the crucified Savior, went with us to as deep depths as He could go that, as the exalted Lord, He might raise us up with Him to the highest heights to which we can go."[11] Therefore, "In Christ we are as far above the power of Satan as Christ is."[12]

> ### Focus on the Victor!
>
> A seasoned pastor, who by God's grace exemplified the epitome of a true prayer warrior, once related to me a series of events that seemed to indicate a satanic attack. It was rather sobering. However, he then emphasized that we do not fear the devil; we fear God. With confidence he said in effect, "We know who the Victor is!" This story beautifully illustrates the importance of focusing on the Victor—the enthroned Christ.
>
> While it is true we need to know biblical truth that exposes the deception of the enemy, it is not true we need to focus on the enemy. True watchfulness is ever looking unto Jesus. Focus on the Victor!

Authority Re-delegated: In this co-resurrection and co-enthronement, God re-delegated authority to man—the church—the body of the Head. Can a body function without the head? I have seen a few chickens at a Colorado ranch try to when beheaded for butchering, but it did not last for long. Does the head function without the body? The answers ought to be obvious. In like manner Christ, the Head, works through His body.

A police officer who is directing traffic would have no power in and of himself to stop oncoming vehicles. But because he wears a badge, he possesses delegated authority, and therefore "power" to stop oncoming traffic. Likewise believers have no power in and of themselves over the enemy. But because of their position in Christ at the throne, they possess delegated authority over the enemy.[13]

3. Comprehend the Privileges of Authority

After comprehending the Person of authority and the position of authority, we must also comprehend the privileges of authority.

The Accessibility of the Privileges of Authority

Ephesians 1:19 specifies "to us-ward who believe." The word "believe" is in the present tense, indicating that which is continuous or repeated. The idea is "to us who keep on believing." The same power which God worked in Christ when He raised Him and exalted Him is available to us, so that victory is secure—since what we face is no greater than raising Christ from the dead and exalting Him far above the enemy. Romans 5:17 affirms that "they which *receive* abundance of grace . . . *reign* in life by one, Jesus Christ."

Responsibility: Often believers think they must ask the Lord to deal with the enemy. While it is most certainly true the authority over the enemy is the Lord's, yet the Lord as the Head delegates to His body the responsibility to exercise authority over the enemy. Jesus explained in Matthew 12:29: "How can one enter into a strong man's house, and spoil his goods, except *he first bind* the strong man? and then he will spoil his house." In Matthew 18:18 Jesus said, "Verily I say unto you, Whatsoever *ye shall bind* on earth shall be bound [literally, shall have been bound] in heaven: and whatsoever ye shall loose on earth shall be loosed [shall have been loosed] in heaven."

Prerequisites: Walking in the light is the way to deal with sin. Walking in the Spirit is the way to keep from sin. Warring from the throne is the way to protect from Satan. Walking in the light (which accesses a clean heart through the cleansing power of the blood) and walking in the Spirit (which accesses a filled life through the enabling power of the Spirit) are the two prerequisites that open the way for warring from the throne (which accesses the throne seat through the authoritative power of the enthroned Christ). The prerequisites of a clean heart and a filled life are not meritorious since they are both matters of faith, as is throne seat authority.

Walking in the light and walking in the Spirit constitute the submission of James 4:7: "Submit yourselves therefore to God," and warring from the throne constitutes the resistance of James 4:7: "Resist the devil, and he will flee from you." The access of "Christ in you" as the provision for the physical realm to deal with the world and the flesh is prerequisite to the access of "you in Christ" as the provision for the spiritual realm to deal with the devil. You cannot claim your position in Christ at the throne when you are walking in the flesh. As Otto Koning observes, "You cannot resist Satan if you are listening to Satan in some way." How foolish for a believer to walk in the flesh and place himself under a defeated foe. But when a believer walks in the Spirit, he can claim his position in Christ at the throne over the enemy. For in the spiritual realm, Satan is at a disadvantage, because he is totally defeated.

Remember the authority of the believer is in the spiritual realm, not the physical realm. The authority is not over human wills, inanimate objects and so forth. Some who are unaware of this boundary may go into excesses that discredit the actual truth. The confusion arises because the spiritual realm often interpenetrates into the physical realm, so that authority exercised in the spiritual realm has ramifications in the physical realm. But the authority of the believer in this present age is only in the spiritual realm.

The Applications of the Privileges of Authority

The privileges of throne seat authority may be applied both defensively and offensively.

Defensively: The believer's position in Christ at the throne is the provision necessary to deal with "fiery darts" (Eph. 6:16). Fiery darts are sinful thoughts or feelings that tempt you to evil yet have no obvious "trigger" in the physical realm. The attack is in the spiritual realm that is invisible yet real. It is as if the powers of darkness hurl a thought or feeling of hatred or impurity or pride into your soul.

However, based on the provision of the believer in Christ far above the enemy, you can lift up the shield of faith and reject the fiery dart. At that moment the dart is quenched—gone from your mind or feelings. This glorious truth will be expanded and illustrated further in chapter 6, "The Overcoming Life."

In addition to fiery darts, there may be times when you just sense the hiss of the serpent at a distance. You can claim your protection in Christ even before the attack becomes close. When you "claim the Name," the authority of the name of Jesus functions like a great "supernatural filter" to guard your inner being.

Also, one individual may access the provision of defense for another. John McMillan, who served as a missionary in China, provides the following account:

> In traveling among the islands off the coast of Mindanao in a native boat, a considerable swell was encountered. The son of the writer began to show fear which became almost uncontrollable. This was most unusual as he was normally fond of the water and was an excellent sailor, having frequently traveled up and down the entire China coast where storms are severe. He begged to be taken ashore, and as the whole affair seemed to be directed against the progress of the evangelistic trip, the writer quietly took the authority of Christ over the spirits of fear and rebuked them, though saying nothing openly. In a very few minutes the lad seemed to change completely, and for the remainder of the journey lasting several days, there was no further difficulty. The second night after, while in the center of a wide bay and about twelve miles from shore, a heavy squall was encountered, and an outrigger broke. The danger was imminent, but, though the lad was fully aware of it, and though the waves were washing quite over the boat, he manifested not the slightest shrinking.[14]

Prudent fathers have the privilege to claim throne seat protection for those under their care. In fact, some apply this privilege every morning and evening.

Believers may together claim their position in Christ at the throne to ward off satanic interference against the work of the Lord. Once while in Cambodia near the Vietnam border, we were preparing to have two evangelistic services at a rural church. However, not far down the road, the Buddhists set up a loudspeaker and, at an exceedingly high volume, played a rather guttural-sounding type of music. It was so loud we knew it would greatly hinder the services. Sensing satanic involvement, several of us banded together to trust the Lord's overruling power. Within minutes the loud speaker stopped altogether. We held two evangelistic services, and there were fifty-seven professions of faith, including a high-ranking elderly Buddhist man who rejoiced greatly at his salvation. Later that night he passed away and went home to be with the Lord.

On two occasions heavy snow was predicted to fall at a time when many people would be traveling to a national conference on revival, and some intercessors claimed throne seat authority over any satanic involvement against the Lord's work. In both cases the weather dissipated dramatically, causing no hindrance. In the first case the news weathermen had predicted blizzard conditions, and they were completely baffled. Attempting to explain how a huge pocket of dry air appeared over the region, they made statements such as, "We don't know where it came from." Praise the Lord—there were those who did!

You do not have to seek opportunity for spiritual warfare, but when you are attacked, it is wonderful to know how to resist the devil based on the truth of God's sure Word: "Submit yourselves therefore to God. Resist the devil, and he will flee from you" (James 4:7).

Offensively: Jesus said, "All power [authority] is given unto me in heaven and in earth. Go ye therefore, and teach [make disciples of] all nations" (Matt. 28:18–20). Paul reminds us under inspiration, "For the weapons of our warfare are not carnal [fleshly], but mighty through God to the pulling down of strongholds" (2 Cor. 10:4).

Strongholds consist of wrong thinking or deception, which hinders right thinking or truth. By this means "the god of this world hath blinded the minds of them which believe not, lest the light of the glorious gospel of Christ, who is the image of God, should shine unto them" (2 Cor. 4:4). In order for people to see the glorious light of gospel truth, strongholds of the enemy must be cast down (2 Cor. 10:5). This gospel offensive occurs through throne seat authority. Individuals or groups of people may exercise this authority.

A lady brought an unsaved cousin to a meeting where I preached. She had witnessed to her often. After the service she witnessed to her again and then invited the pastor and me into the conversation. The unsaved lady had a son who had committed suicide. Because of this, she considered herself to be a murderer and thought she could not get saved. We explained that the power and love of Jesus reaches even to murderers, and we gave the example of Saul of Tarsus who consented to the murder of Stephen. However, every sensible biblical argument we mentioned seemed to have no penetrating effect at all.

Recognizing the stronghold the enemy built up in this dear lady's mind, I suggested we all get down on our knees to pray. Through exercising throne seat authority, the scales of blindness fell off of this lady's eyes. Then she could see the glorious light of the gospel. When again pointed to Jesus' offer of salvation, she gladly responded to the invitation to trust in Jesus to save her, and she rejoiced with joy unspeakable.

This same dynamic is needed for multitudes without Christ. The prayer meeting of Acts 1 accessed the outpouring of the Spirit of Acts 2. This is an example of greater works—the powers of darkness dispelled and the power of the Spirit displayed—so that many have the opportunity to hear "the word of the Lord" in a setting where it has "free course" and is "glorified" or given its full weight (2 Thess. 3:1). Jesus said,

> Verily, verily, I say unto you, He that believeth on me, the works that I do shall he do also; and greater works than these shall he do; because I go unto my Father [the throne seat]. And whatsoever ye shall ask in my name [authority], that will I do, that the Father may be glorified in the Son. If ye shall ask anything in my name [authority], I will do it. (John 14:12–14)

Whether individually or corporately, whether defensively or offensively, learn to claim the Name—the name of Jesus! This is not a mere mantra of words. When the Spirit convinces you of the truth of the enthroned Christ, you can claim the Name and experience throne seat authority!

> O claim the Name—the Name of Jesus,
> The Name that is above all names;
> O claim the Name—the Name of Jesus,
> That overrules all other claims.[15]

We have examined the provisions of the Christ life in the last few chapters. When the Spirit convinces you of the abundant provision available, you must access your inheritance in Christ. We are about to discover the key turning point that can bring you into the glorious freedom God intends.

· · · · ·

Questions for Personal Reflection

1. How has your vision of Christ been expanded by focusing on His enthronement?

2. How has your faith been nurtured regarding being in Christ at the throne?

3. In what common ways do you sense a need to apply throne seat authority defensively and offensively?

5

THE SURRENDER EXCHANGE

How to Make the Exchange

I beseech you therefore, brethren, by the mercies of God, that ye present your bodies a living sacrifice, holy, acceptable unto God, which is your reasonable service. And be not conformed to this world: but be ye transformed by the renewing of your mind, that ye may prove what is that good, and acceptable, and perfect, will of God. ROMANS 12:1–2

ONCE, while holding meetings on the coast of Maine, we visited picturesque Camden Harbor. As we walked along the dock, advertisements for various cruises constantly vied for our attention. In one window I noticed a handwritten sign advertising a boat rental for ten dollars. The low price grabbed my attention, and I assumed the sign referred to the small but good-looking boats with fairly large engines docked nearby. I promised my son I would take him later that week on a boat ride to Curtis Island to see the lighthouse there.

When we returned for the boat ride, I discovered that the boats I had seen were those used by yacht owners to get to their yachts. The ten-dollar (per hour) rental price was for a little dinghy, or rowboat. When I asked how long it would take to row to Curtis Island, the man working with us casually said, "Oh, about twenty minutes." That sounded workable. So paying the money and putting on our life vests, my son and I made our way to the dinghy.

The paint was chipped, and the wood was somewhat rotten, but we stepped in and got ourselves situated. Having a city-kid background, I knew very little about rowing. I found it worked best to row with my body facing the opposite direction we were headed. This meant my son, six years old at the time, became the navigator.

Pushing away from the dock, we began our journey. Sometimes the metal rings that held the oars in place would pop out of the rotting wood, inevitably altering our direction. Sometimes I would put too much effort into one oar over the other—this sent us in circles! I'm sure we were great entertainment for any who might be watching.

Traveling along the edge of the harbor to stay out of the way of large sea vessels, and zigzagging through a parking lot of sailboats, we finally arrived at Curtis Island—45 minutes later. After an enjoyable time exploring the island and visiting the lighthouse, I endured another 45 minutes of laborious rowing.

Just as I ended up rowing in circles when I overused one oar, some believers make no real progress on their spiritual journey. They end up going in circles because they are using only one oar of spiritual truth. To progress on the journey, you must use both oars.

Romans 12:1–2 describes full surrender—what we might call "a two-oared surrender." This full surrender involves a full exchange, a "surrender exchange" in which we must participate. But what does this mean? This classic passage in Romans answers that question by emphasizing two main points and delineating several minor points that complete the concept of full surrender.

The Main Points of Surrender

What does it mean to "use both oars"? William Boardman wrote, "The experience of the higher Christian life is the same as conversion in two essential ways: First, *Christ is all-sufficient*, and second, *faith is all-inclusive*."[16] The second point, all-inclusive faith, is based on the first, Christ's all-sufficiency.

We have focused on the cleansing power of Christ's blood, the enabling power of Christ's Spirit and the authoritative power of Christ's throne. Truly the Lord Jesus Christ is an all-sufficient Savior! His all-sufficiency is our provision. But this provision must be accessed by an all-inclusive faith—or we might say "a two-oared faith." Since Christ is all-sufficient, faith must be all-inclusive.

The all-inclusiveness of faith demands the use of the two oars of surrender to maintain real progress. As Boardman stated it, "Let either element of faith be lacking, and the soul is like a boat with only one oar, going round and round but making no progress."[17] Full surrender involves a full exchange. Without this full exchange, frustration and defeat will mark your life. With this full exchange, revival blessing will mark your life.

What are the two oars of a full surrender, the two oars of an all-inclusive faith? What comprises a full exchange? Romans 12:1–2 tells us.

1. Give Your All to Jesus

The main point of Romans 12:1 is to "*present* your bodies a living sacrifice." Give your all to Jesus, trusting Him to take it. This "give all" is an *active presentation* that surrenders entirely to Christ's *leadership*. This first choice embraces *the will of God* for your life in all matters. It embraces the purpose of God with a heart motivated to please Him and Him alone. When you present your all to Jesus as a living sacrifice, you are abandoning yourself to the *lordship* of Jesus Christ.

2. Take Christ's All to You

The main point of Romans 12:2 is to be "*transformed* by the renewing of your mind." Take Christ's all to you, trusting Him to give it. This "take all" is an *allowed transformation* that surrenders entirely to Christ's *enabling power*. This second choice embraces *the way of God* for your life in all matters. When you take His all to you, and thus allow yourself to be transformed, you are abandoning yourself to the *life* of Christ.

The verb "transformed" is passive, indicating the obedience to this command is not something *you do*, but something you allow *to be done to you*. This same word is translated "transfigured" in the Gospels. When Christ was transfigured, He allowed the glory of His deity to radiate. Who He is—deity—was manifested. When you allow yourself to be transformed, who you are—Christ in you, the hope of glory—is manifested. This is personal revival, for revival is a restoration to life—Christ's life.

The full exchange of full surrender involves yielding all to Christ and finding all in Christ. Giving your all to Jesus actually means to trust Him as your leader; taking Christ's all to you actually means to trust Him as your enabler.

Clarifications

It may be helpful to clarify in more detail why it is vital to apply both main points.

The Problem of Giving All without Taking All

How many have tried to surrender all to God yet have been frustrated and defeated? They sincerely pray, "God, I surrender all!" But nothing seems to change. The problem is using only one oar. They surrender to God's will (the best they know), but they trust in themselves to carry it out. In other words, they fail to depend on God's power. They give their all to Jesus, but they fail to take His all to them.

Essentially, this fallacious thinking says, "I surrender all— and *I'm* going to do it!" I fell into this deception in my early years. But you and I can't do it. Therefore, when we depend on Christ's leadership, we must also depend on His enabling power to follow His leadership. If you say, "I surrender all, and I'm going to do it," you have not surrendered all. While you have surrendered to God's will, you have not surrendered to His power.

Surrendering to Christ's enabling power involves *giving up* your strength by *giving in* to God's strength. Full surrender means trusting in the Spirit as *life*, as well as yielding to the Spirit as *Lord*. Otherwise you end up with "consecrated self." This is the mistake of flesh-dependent obedience. It is not self-indulgence in the works of the flesh, but it is self-dependence in the work (strength) of the flesh.

Yet Jesus clearly says, "It is the spirit [Spirit] that quickeneth [gives life]; the flesh profiteth nothing" (John 6:63). He later affirms, "Without me, ye can do nothing" (15:5). With Christ, "I can do all things through Christ which strengtheneth me" (Phil. 4:13). But without Him we can only produce "wood, hay," and "stubble" (1 Cor. 3:11–15).

Surrender is not "a commitment to obey God." As good as that phrase may sound, your "commitment to obey" leaves you as the power source. Yet the reality is we are weak. The concept of full surrender recognizes this fact. Well do I remember when the Spirit sank the truth down deep into my heart: "I'm weak, and I will always be weak this side of heaven. But He's strong, and He will always be strong. The Spirit-filled life is not me becoming strong; it is me recognizing that I am weak and always will be, so I keep trusting in Him who is always strong." What a life-changing revelation!

Surrender is not only giving up your will; surrender is giving up your strength (which is actually weakness) as well. When you think it is your job to be victorious, you are using only one oar, and you will make no progress. If there is some sin issue that seems too great for you to overcome, and you shrink back into thinking you have to live with that besetting sin, then you are viewing the issue from the perspective of your strength rather than God's. But the issue is no match for the Spirit of Christ in you to overcome. Exchange your strength for Christ's strength, and He will impart to you His victorious life. It is not your job to be victorious—it is Christ's! Jesus Christ is the victory—the victorious life Himself. Therefore, when you give your all to Him, take His all to you.

"But thanks be to God, which giveth [is giving] us the victory through our Lord Jesus Christ" (1 Cor. 15:57). Since He *is giving* to us His victory, let's *be taking* His victory. The battles of conquest will rise on life's horizon, but "the battle is the LORD's" (1 Sam. 17:47). Take His all to you, and you will find Him to be what He is—all-sufficient.

If you do not use this second oar along with the first, you will eventually despair, because you will learn that you can't live victoriously by your own power. William Boardman paints the picture: "But at some point we see the Canaanites—the giant sins in the walled cities of our hearts. And when we think of conquering them, we see it is *our* job, not the Lord's, and we shrink from it as hopeless. We content ourselves as well as we can with a life of wandering in the wilderness, simply because we fail to move forward in faith to victory, trusting in God alone to give it."[18]

Let your mind be renewed in the truth: Christ is giving to you the victory (1 Cor. 15:57), and Christ is living in you (Gal. 2:20). As you depend on Christ's leadership, depend also on His enabling power, and He will transform your living sacrifice by His very own life.

The Problem of Taking All without Giving All

But the reverse can also be problematic. How many have tried to trust God for His power and yet have been frustrated and defeated? They take His all to them, but nothing seems to change. Again the problem is using only one oar. Only this time it's the other oar. Some surrender to God's way by trusting in His power, but they do so in an attempt to accomplish their own will, not God's. In other words, they fail to surrender to God's will. They take Christ's all to them, but they fail to give their all to Him.

Essentially, this fallacious thinking says, "Lord, here's my plan. Please give me the power to carry it out. Here's what I am trying to do for You, Lord. Now please bless it." This is dependence on God—for our purposes. But who is in charge? We are most certainly to trust in God, but for His purposes, not our own, even if they are good things. To trust in Him merely in an attempt to accomplish your plans, will again produce the frustration of circular motion with no progress.

The Scripture makes clear, "yield yourselves *unto God*, as those that are alive from the dead, and your members as instruments of righteousness *unto God*" (Rom. 6:13). Since Jesus is Lord, from the center to the circumference of your being, give your all to Him. This is the first main point: "present your bodies a living sacrifice." This first point of surrendering to Christ's leadership is vital for the second point of surrendering to His enabling power to have effect.

We need the balance of both main points. We must use both oars. Give your all to Jesus, trusting Him to take it. Take His all to you, trusting Him to give it. Give all *and* take all.

In other words, exchange your all for His all. What an unbeatable exchange! The surrender exchange leads to real progress and growth in grace.

The Minor Points of Surrender

Romans 12:1–2 delineates several lesser points of surrender as well. As points of truth they are important, but they are subordinate to the main points.

The Object of Surrender

Since the text says we are to present all "unto God," the object of the surrender is God. Although the text does not specify which person of the Godhead, it is the Holy Spirit who indwells your body. Technically, there is a sense in which the object of the surrender is to the Holy Spirit. Yet the Holy Spirit is the Spirit of the Father and the Spirit of the Son. On this basis the Scripture legitimately says, "the Holy Spirit which is in you" (1 Cor. 6:19) and "Christ in you" (Col. 1:27), and so forth. As a result, we may speak of surrendering to God the Father, to Jesus Christ or to the Holy Spirit.

The Faith of Surrender

Surrender and faith properly understood are two sides of one coin. When you surrender to Christ's leadership, you are depending on His leadership. Or when you depend on Christ's leadership, you are surrendering to His leadership. Similarly, when you surrender to Christ's enabling power, you are depending on His power. Or when you depend on Christ's enabling power, you are surrendering to His power. Though distinguishable in emphasis, surrender and faith are two expressions of one essential truth. Surrender properly understood is dependence, and dependence properly understood is surrender.

Often people use the word "surrender" when referring to *leadership* and the word "faith" when referring to *enabling*. However, more accurately, it is the surrender of faith or the faith of surrender involving two vital areas: leadership (God's will) and enabling (God's way). As we have discussed, these two vital areas comprise the two oars of surrender/faith.

The Responsibility of Surrender

Since the Scripture "beseeches" us to surrender, the surrender exchange is a responsibility, not that which is inevitable. Tragically, many miss this profound dynamic and become fatalistic regarding God's provision. "I beseech *you* . . . that *ye* present . . ." shows us that surrender demands active cooperation, not passive resignation. The text could not be clearer. The nature of surrender/faith is a responsibility.

Waving the white flag of surrender indicates *giving up* by *giving in*. This is not passive resignation, which would make you dead weight. If you did not actively cooperate with your conqueror, you would probably become actual "dead" weight! Making the surrender exchange involves surrendering your will and way to God's will and way. You give up by giving in. This is faith, or dependence, on the Spirit's leadership and power. But unlike a wartime surrender which would be a begrudging surrender, the surrender exchange is a glad surrender based on the loving provision of a loving Deliverer.

We are not speaking of passivity, which would be "will-ing" yourself into "will-lessness." Passivity is the devil's playground. Satan demands a passive instrument, whereas the Holy Spirit demands an active, cooperating instrument. Satan works around your faculties, whereas the Holy Spirit works through your cooperating faculties. Surrender/faith is not idle passivity, it is active cooperation. It is a matter of exercising your will, not for your own purposes but for God's.

The Totality of Surrender

"That ye present your *bodies*" reveals a total surrender since your body encompasses the totality of your being. However, if "your body is the temple of the Holy Ghost which is in you" (1 Cor. 6:19), why then does Romans 12:1 beseech you to present your body? Technically, when the Holy Spirit moved in to you at salvation, He moved into your spirit. Romans 12:1 beseeches you to present "the rest of you" to the Spirit for full hands-on possession. This is not a matter of you getting more of the Holy Spirit but rather a matter of the Holy Spirit getting more of you.

Suppose a guest comes into your house and you show him to the guest room. Would you then lock him in? Yet this is essentially what many do to the Holy Spirit. For example, when the Holy Spirit seeks to go in to the kitchen of your appetites (and I'm not just speaking of food), do you seek to block Him from entering, as if He does not already know what is there? When the Spirit seeks to open up a closet, do you seek to block Him from seeing the skeleton in the closet, as if He does not already know about it? If you act like you are in charge of even one closet, you are not surrendered; you are acting like your own master.

While there is a sense in which the Spirit is in charge whether you recognize His lordship or not, you must recognize it in order to benefit according to God's design. Is it not amazing that God in His sovereign wisdom beseeches us to present all to Him? We are not robots. God wants us to lovingly trust Him by giving all to Him. The totality of the surrender of Romans 12:1 simply gives "the whole house" to the indwelling Christ for full possession.

In some cultures it is possible to purchase a particular product, to take the title deed in hand, and yet not to have the product delivered for several weeks. When you trusted Christ, He, who purchased you with His own blood, took the title deed of your life in hand. He owns you. Full surrender simply delivers to Him what He already owns for full, hands-on possession.

The Timing of Surrender

Full surrender begins with a definite presentation leading to a daily process. The phrase "that ye present yourselves a living sacrifice" highlights both concepts.

First, the verb "present" indicates the fact of an action or a definite event. The starting point of full surrender is this definite presentation. It need not be dramatic, but it ought to be definite. Second, the participle "living" indicates continuous action. The starting point of surrender is just that—a starting point. The definite presentation simply begins the daily process of continual cooperation with the Spirit's purpose and power.

Some liken the Spirit-filled life to driving a car. But often they mistakenly think, "I'll just turn the steering wheel of my life over to the Holy Spirit." While this may sound good as an analogy to the definite presentation, it leaves out the daily process. If the Holy Spirit took over the wheel, then from that point on everything would be automatic and perfect. But obviously, that is not how it works, for it leaves out the continual cooperation God intended.

When my father used to teach about the Holy Spirit, he used the analogy of a car in this way: the Holy Spirit says to the believer, "You stay behind the wheel; just do everything I say." This reveals the daily process of absolute surrender. You and I have the privilege of being chauffeurs of deity. When the Spirit says, "Turn right, stop, go, turn that television program off, throw away that DVD or CD, don't wear that, forgive, give that person a gospel tract, speak, declare the gospel," and so forth, yield to the Spirit's navigation. He is greater than any navigation system of man.

The timing of surrender is *all the time*—a definite presentation, leading to a daily process.

The Acceptance of Surrender

If you give your all to Jesus, will He accept it? And if so, why? Our text says this surrender is "holy, acceptable unto God." Who does what? You surrender and God sanctifies, as is seen in the phrase "holy [sanctified] . . . unto God." We have already noted

Crisis and Process

Some who embrace sanctification by faith, sometimes known as Keswick theology, teach concerning surrender the concept of "crisis and process," or more specifically a crisis leading to a process. Surrender is not once for all, in the sense of never needing further surrender, but it is stepping onto the path of surrender. Stepping onto the path of surrender (crisis) leads to walking in surrender (process).

However, others misunderstand what is meant by the word *crisis*. Rightly understood, the crisis is simply the presentation of Romans 12:1. It is the directional surrender that begins a life of faith in earnest. It is the starting point from which the process of daily surrender follows. It need not be a dramatic experience, but it must be definite—just as salvation need not be dramatic but must be definite. While this can coincide with one's moment of salvation, for many it comes later. This explains why Paul, under inspiration, beseeches the "brethren" (those who are already Christians) to "present" (crisis) their bodies a "living" (process) sacrifice.

that we cannot consecrate ourselves. But when you surrender, God consecrates, or sanctifies, what you surrender. Also, you give and God takes, as is seen in the phrase "acceptable unto God." Since God sanctifies the gift, He also accepts the gift. What an amazing reality—God *accepts* the gift of full surrender! Therefore, give your all to Jesus, *trusting Him to take it.*

To further prove the acceptance of your presentation, after you have given your all to Jesus, take His all to you, trusting Him to give it—for He is giving His all to you when you are following His leadership.

The Logic of Surrender

The surrender exchange is logical because the text states, "which is your reasonable service." What God beseeches of His children is rational.

It is logical because of His *mercies.* Romans 12:1 begins by saying, "I beseech you therefore, brethren, by *the mercies of God,* that . . ." The preceding chapters of Romans 1–11 form the doctrinal emphasis as the basis for the practical emphasis of Romans 12–16. These "mercies" include the doctrine of justification by faith (Rom. 1–5), the doctrine of sanctification by faith (Rom. 6–8) and God's system of "by grace, through faith" (Rom. 9–11).

Surrender is logical because of His *ownership.* The Scripture is clear: "*ye are not your own* . . . ye are bought with a price: therefore glorify God in your body, and in your spirit, *which are God's*" (1 Cor. 6:19–20). Missions pioneer C.T. Studd wrote,

> I had known about Jesus Christ's dying for me, but I had never understood that if He died for me, then I didn't belong to myself. When I came to see that Jesus Christ had died for me, it didn't seem hard to give up all for HIM. It just seemed common ordinary honesty. . . . I realized that my life was to

be one of simple, child-like faith. . . . I was to trust in Him that He would work in me to do His good pleasure.[19]

Studd, from a wealthy home and already a famous athlete, considered it theft not to surrender all. It was logical to walk away from career, fame and fortune, for he understood he had been purchased and was no longer his own. Have you faced the logic of surrender?

The surrender exchange is also logical because of Christ's *offer*. When you give your all to Jesus, you may take His all to you. This is similar to a bride who gives her all to her groom, but she also gets to take his all to her. Yet for us the contrast is far more striking. Our all is ultimately nothing, for apart from Christ we can do nothing (John 15:5). Yet the invitation is offered: "Ho, every one that thirsteth, come ye to the waters, and he that hath no money; come ye, buy, and eat; yea, come, buy wine and milk without money and without price" (Isa. 55:1). Exchange your nothingness for His fullness. What an unbeatable exchange!

The Point of Surrender

Some may wonder if surrender is simply saying, "I surrender all." It can be if you understand what that means. However, often surrender is more practical than that. Often it demands yielding on what we might call a given "point of surrender." The point of surrender is whatever you are saying no to God about. It is a point of resisting God, or being reticent to even "go there," thus revealing a heart that is not surrendered.

The point of surrender is a particular love that is not of God. First John 2:15–16 admonishes, "Love not the world, neither the things that are in the world. If any man love the world, the love of [for] the Father is not in him. For all that is in the world, the lust of the flesh, and the lust of the eyes, and the pride of life, is not of the Father, but it is of the world." The phrase "the lust of the flesh" addresses physical desire that goes beyond God's boundaries. Is there a point of surrender here? The phrase "the lust of the eyes" addresses material desire that becomes a matter of covetousness and violates good stewardship. Is there a point of surrender here? The phrase "the pride of life" addresses egotistical desire that may be expressed in wrong motivations. Perhaps it is a dream, an ambition that is not God's will for you, and either feeds the desire for status or simply feeds the "this is what I want" part of the flesh. Perhaps it is resentment you savor, or even a desire for revenge that expresses or feeds bitterness, that takes satisfaction in putting another down as you lift yourself up. These are all loves that are a part of the world—the world system under the influence of the god of this world.

It should be no surprise that in the midst of two classic Bible verses on surrender we find the command, "And be not conformed to this world." The grammar incorporated often conveys the idea of "*Stop* being pressed into the mold of this evil age." Before you can be *trans*formed you have to stop being *con*formed. As one preacher friend honestly admitted, "Worldliness saps me spiritually."

But this is not a matter of replacing one kind of conformity with another. If you do, then you are supposedly "giving all to Jesus," but you are definitely missing "taking His all to you." It is replacing being conformed to this world with being transformed by the Spirit.

The point of surrender will vary from person to person. In a church where I was holding meetings, a new convert of six months said to the pastor and me that he had gotten rid of some DVDs. He said he was a "Hollywood buff" and regularly purchased new Hollywood movies. Then he said honestly, "But they make me backslide. So today I got rid of six hundred DVDs!"

Sometimes the issue will be less obvious. A real test of surrender may involve that which good men debate over but the Holy Spirit says to you, "Give it up." When this occurs, the debate ought to be over *for you*. If you argue that the issue is not a big deal ("It's just one DVD" or "It's only one article of clothing") and seek to excuse it because good men debate about it, then you are saying no to the Holy Spirit's leadership *for you*. This is a big deal. What may seem like a small issue really is a big issue when it becomes the point of surrender. If you say no, you just cut yourself off from the Spirit-filled life—the Spirit filling you with the life of Christ.

A pastor once told me on a Monday night that he and his wife went home on Sunday evening and gave up a particular television program they had enjoyed watching, because the Spirit had convicted them about it. Then he testified he had a wonderful day; it was as if he got sensitized to the Holy Spirit, and the Spirit was more real to him. He said, "I know this would not have been the case if I had said no last night." By the end of the week, he was in personal revival and commented, "I cringe to think what I would have missed if I had said no on Sunday night!" Today he is years down the revival road.

Is there anything you are saying no to God about? Give it up. This is surrender/faith regarding the Spirit's leadership.

The Demonstration of Surrender

Romans 12:1–2 concludes with, "that ye may prove what is that good, and acceptable, and perfect, will of God." The surrender exchange "proves" or demonstrates the perfect will of God—that which is good, acceptable and perfect. In other words, since the surrender exchange is a matter of faith, it is the opportunity for God to demonstrate Himself. Faith is not a work; it is dependence upon the Worker. When this occurs, the Worker—God

Himself—is demonstrated. Surrender allows for a demonstration of God's will and God's power.

Early in the 1990s we ministered in a church that has invited us back regularly ever since. The first time we went there, I noticed a particular man who carried a scowl on his face, seemed uninterested in the preaching and was quite difficult to work with. He was this way for a number of years. Then at one of our return meetings, I could not help but see a great change in him. He glowed with the radiance of the indwelling Christ, devoured the preaching and was a joy to work with. This change has now lasted for a number of years. What happened? He accessed the Christ life through the surrender exchange and is being transformed by the power of the Spirit.

It is amazing what God will do when you give your all to Jesus, trusting Him to take it, and you take His all to you, trusting Him to give it. Will you make the exchange? Will you "put both oars in the water"? Once the surrender exchange is real, you are equipped for the overcoming life.

• • • • •

Questions for Personal Reflection

1. If you think you are surrendered but have been frustrated by a lack of progress spiritually, which oar of surrender is lacking?

2. What point or points of surrender came to mind, if any, regarding the practical reality of truly surrendering all?

3. What new surrenders are you presently facing?

6

THE OVERCOMING LIFE

How to Take the Way of Escape in the Face of Temptation

There hath no temptation taken you but such as is common to man: but God is faithful, who will not suffer you to be tempted above that ye are able; but will with the temptation also make a way to escape, that ye may be able to bear it. 1 CORINTHIANS 10:13

IN the late 1960s our family left Chicago for a vacation in Durango, Colorado. Driving southwest from Denver, we traveled on Highway 160 over Wolf Creek Pass in the Rocky Mountains. I remember it as a narrow, two-lane road, often with no shoulders or guardrails. As the fourth in a family of five siblings, I was relegated to the back seat of the station wagon.

Winding our way up Wolf Creek Pass, the older siblings, having a little fun, said things to scare the younger ones. As we climbed higher through the mountains, the steep cliffs terrified me. Riding in the inside lane near the mountain wall was some comfort, as we were farther from the edge. But as the curves switched directions, riding in the outside lane was horrifying; often it seemed you looked straight down great distances into the ravines and valleys below.

Finally we crested the top of Wolf Creek Pass and began to wind our way back down. Every so often you would see a strategically placed escape ramp for heavy vehicles that might suffer brake failure. Without those ramps, drivers who lost their brakes could be thrust off the mountainside at a sharp curve and plunge below to near-certain death.

As we made our way through this section, all of a sudden my parents and older siblings gasped with horror at what obviously was no longer a joke. Seeing everyone looking down off one side of our car, I put my little face in the window and followed their line of gaze. Hundreds of feet below an eighteen-wheeler lay smashed at the bottom of a ravine. More than likely the driver had been killed in the tragic crash—evidently because he failed to take the way of escape.

First Corinthians 10:6–10 mentions the common temptations of craving evil things, idolatry, immorality, maligning God and complaining. But in verse thirteen God promises to faithfully provide a way of escape. Actually, a definite article precedes the word "way," indicating that God faithfully provides *the* way to escape. We must learn to always take the way of escape to experience the overcoming life. But how can we be sure not to miss God's escape ramps? First Corinthians 10:13 provides two areas of truth that must be embraced and applied.

Customized Provision

God promises that when we face temptation, He will "*make* [the] way to escape." There is a sense in which God customizes the way of escape. God will provide the way of escape according to the type of temptation you are facing on the road of life. Broadly, temptation comes through the world, the flesh and/or the devil. But specifically, there are three approaches the world, the flesh and the devil use. These approaches determine which provision or "escape ramp" you will need.

Temptation through Apparent Causes

Much temptation has apparent causes; it approaches through the world and the flesh—the realm of what is seen, heard, touched, smelled and tasted. Temptation of this sort arises from the physical realm. Therefore, this type of temptation is not necessarily a direct attack from the enemy. In other words, though apparent causes trigger the temptation, it does not necessarily follow that a demon is sitting by each apparent cause. Rather, these are indirect attacks from the enemy utilizing worldly or fleshly snares.

When a hunter sets a trap or snare, he does not sit down right by it and wait for an animal to come. Obviously, he leaves the area, counting on the trap or snare to do its work. Then he returns later to check on it. Similarly, Satan is a master hunter. He and his cohorts of evil set traps and snares in this world system, and they know from millenniums of practice what appeals to the flesh of mankind. But they do not need to maintain a presence by each trap or snare; they often simply count on the traps and snares to do their work.

For example, the hosts of evil will use various forms of advertising to trigger temptation to covetousness, vice and impure thinking. When this kind of temptation draws you, you know where it's coming from. The source is quite apparent.

How about irritating circumstances that trigger the temptation to impatience or anger? Perhaps you stub your toe or the corner of a table digs into your thigh; maybe a co-worker makes an abrasive comment or the neighbor's children are too noisy. In all such cases the source of the temptation is apparent.

There are many other examples of such temptations: the sight of an attractive woman may trigger the temptation to lust; the smell of a particular food may trigger the temptation to gluttony; the sound of a few flattering words may trigger the temptation to pride. All these arise from an apparent cause.

Deliverance from Apparent-Cause Temptation

When apparent causes trigger the temptation, two biblical truths form the foundation of faith for overcoming the temptation: *the person of divine ability*—Christ in you—and *the principle of counteraction*.

First, *the person of divine ability* is emphasized in biblical phrases like "Christ, who is our life" (Col. 3:4) and "I live, yet not I, but Christ" by "faith" (Gal. 2:20). As noted in the chapter on "The Exchanged Life," believers have been severed from indwelling sin and joined to the indwelling Christ. Christ in the believer is *the victorious life*. He is *the overcoming life* Himself. What a blessed provision of divine ability!

Second, *the principle of counteraction* is emphasized factually in the statement, "For the law of the Spirit of life in Christ Jesus hath made me free from the law of sin and death" (Rom. 8:2) and functionally in the promise, "If ye through the Spirit do mortify the deeds of the body, ye shall live" (Rom. 8:13). The greater "law of the Spirit" counteracts and overcomes the lesser "law of sin" when you "through the Spirit" face the temptations that appeal to "the deeds of the body." The promise is clear: "through the Spirit . . . ye shall live." What a blessed promise of victorious counteraction!

But the provision of what is (Christ living in you) and the promise of what *will be* (overcoming physical temptation) demand faith. Our responsibility is to exercise faith in Christ to overcome temptation by appropriating or taking Christ's divine ability to counteract and overcome the world and the flesh. Take the provision to overcome the temptation based on the promise. Simply put, trust to obey.

Appropriation is like taking money out of your checking account. When you go to your bank to withdraw money held in your checking account, you do not have to give an emotional and eloquent speech to retrieve your money. As long as you have your account number and money in your account, you have the right to draw from your bank account. Similarly, when you received Christ, you received the inexhaustible bank account of heaven. You may appropriate—take—what is already yours in Christ for whatever needs you may face.

Counteraction is like corrective lenses. I am near-sighted. Without my glasses, my vision blurs the details of what is actually before me. But when I put on my glasses, my vision clears. You might say "the law of corrective lenses" counteracts and overcomes "the law of nearsightedness." However, this does not cure my vision. As soon as I take off my glasses, my vision blurs again. But as long as I depend on my glasses, the law of corrective lenses overcomes the law of nearsightedness. Similarly, when you take the provision of Christ's divine ability, He imparts to you His divine life to easily counteract and overcome the temptation you are facing in the earthly realm of the world and the flesh.

For example, when a billboard tempts you to impure thoughts, simply declare with confidence, "Thank you, Lord, for Your purity," and He liberates you to look the other way and be free from the temptation—as if you never saw it. When an irritating circumstance tempts you to impatience, declare from the heart, "Thank you, Lord, for Your patience," and He supernaturally enables you to respond with His patience. When an abrasive comment tempts you to harshness, lift the heart cry,

"Thank you, Lord, for Your love," and He imparts to you His divine love.

Once when tempted to despise someone I found hard to love, I cried out in my heart, "Your love, Lord," and immediately my whole perspective toward that person was altered as the love of God was shed abroad in my heart.

To keep matters real simple, whatever the temptation is, just declare from your heart, "Thank you, Lord, for Your life." For His life covers every situation, and there is a sense in which the gift is not separate from the Giver. This is the provision of divine ability to be victorious in the physical realm.

Temptation through Non-Apparent Causes

But how do you handle approaching temptation when there is no apparent cause—attacks directly from the powers of darkness?

Sometimes we find ourselves tempted even though nothing in the physical realm—the realm of the senses—triggers the temptation. Temptation of this sort arises from the spiritual realm—the realm where evil spirits work. These are direct attacks from the enemy to your soul, especially your mind and/or your emotions. The Bible calls such attacks "fiery darts" (Eph. 6:16).

For example, a feeling of discouragement may slowly pervade your mood without any apparent cause. Suppose you start the day in the Word and prayer, not just ritualistically but really meeting with God. Then you go to work with a song in your heart. But about three hours later you become aware of the feeling of discouragement. Stop and consider if an apparent cause is the source. If nothing comes to mind, then recognize you are dealing with a fiery dart.

Sometimes a spiritual dullness may come over you like a creeping fog. Yet when you ask God to search your heart, no sin issue comes to mind. This indicates you are dealing with a fiery dart.

Perhaps you are in a particular thought pattern in your work or at home, and suddenly other unrelated thoughts come cruising across your brain—thoughts of hatred, pride or impurity—and you think to yourself, *Where did that come from?* Again, recognize the fiery darts thrown by the powers of darkness in an attempt to penetrate your soul.

A Christian man once told me he attended an evangelistic service I preached. The subject that night was on the realities of hell. He said he wanted to hear every word spoken. Yet all of a sudden in the middle of the message, vile thoughts began to bombard his mind. He then asked, "Do you think that could have been from the devil?" Remember, he was in the middle of an evangelistic service, the message was on hell, and he wanted to listen. Obviously, there was no apparent cause for his temptation. This was a direct attack of fiery darts. It was not a case of walking through a shopping mall where there might be an apparent cause for the temptation from store displays or immodestly dressed people.

Deliverance from Non-Apparent-Cause Temptation

When temptation approaches through non-apparent causes, two biblical truths form the foundation of faith for overcoming the temptation: *the position of divine authority*—you in Christ—and *the principle of counterattack*. This is a different provision for a different attack. It is important to recognize where the attack is coming from so that you may apply the appropriate truth. If you apply truth that does not seem to work in a given situation, it reveals you are not applying the appropriate truth. This is what I mean by a "customized provision."

First, *the position of divine authority* is emphasized in Ephesians 1 and 2, as we noted in the chapter entitled "The Throne Seat."

> And what is the exceeding greatness of his power to us-ward who believe, according to the working of his mighty power, which he wrought in Christ, when he raised him from the dead, and set him at his own right hand in the heavenly places, far above all principality, and power, and might, and dominion, and every name that is named, not only in this world, but also in that which is to come. . . . And hath raised us up together, and made us sit together in heavenly places in Christ Jesus. (Eph. 1:19–21; 2:6)

God displayed His mighty power "when he raised him from the dead . . . and hath raised us up together," for the Head must of necessity be raised with the body, and when He "set him at his own right hand in the heavenly places [the authority of the throne] . . . and made us sit together in heavenly places in Christ Jesus." Through salvation, God identifies believers in Christ's death, burial, resurrection and *enthronement*. What a blessed provision of divine authority!

Second, *the principle of counterattack* is emphasized in the statement, "Above all, taking the shield of faith, wherewith ye shall be able to quench all the fiery darts of the wicked [one]" (Eph. 6:16). The "shield of faith" quenches or counters successfully all the fiery darts hurled by the powers of darkness. What a blessed promise of counterattack!

But the provision of what *is* (you in Christ at the throne of authority) and the promise of what *will be* (overcoming spiritual temptation) demand faith. Our responsibility is to exercise faith in Christ to overcome temptation by appropriating, or taking, Christ's divine authority to counterattack and overrule the foe. Claim your protection in Christ at the throne and exercise delegated authority to extinguish the fiery darts.

Appropriation in this case is like the police officer directing traffic through delegated authority. So you may exercise Christ's authority over the powers of darkness. You may appropriate—

take—your position in Christ at the throne to deal with the satanic attack.

"The shield of faith" lifted in defense pictures counterattack because it accesses divine authority to "quench" or extinguish fiery darts. If the shield of faith only deflected fiery darts, soon you would be enveloped in flames. But the shield of faith actually puts the fire out by extinguishing the fiery darts. When you lift the shield of faith, claiming your position in Christ and exercising His authority over the powers of darkness, the enemy must flee.

For example, when you recognize the fiery dart of discouragement, simply declare in confidence, "I claim my position in Christ at the throne, and I reject this feeling of discouragement." Immediately the dart dissipates—it's gone. This is claiming the authoritative name of Jesus based on truth.

When spiritual dullness is not on account of sin or partial confession, simply declare from your heart, "I claim the name of Jesus, and I reject this feeling of dullness." Once while in a local church revival meeting, two men lamented about feeling spiritually dull when they attempted to read their Bible and pray each morning. I questioned if they had asked the Lord to search their hearts to see if some sin hindered. They both said they had, but nothing came to mind. Then we discussed the scriptural truth of dealing with fiery darts. Later in the week they both testified that they claimed their authority in Christ and rejected the satanic attack, and both radiantly testified to reveling for the past several days in their time with God.

If unwanted thoughts break into your thought process, simply declare, "I claim my protection in Christ, and I reject these thoughts." Immediately you will sense a lift in your spirit, as the fiery darts are supernaturally quenched. The name of Jesus is above all names!

The Spirit-filled Life and Spiritual Warfare

When you enter the Spirit-filled life with understanding, you have entered the *spiritual realm*. This is a different realm than what you were used to. The hosts of evil will likely attempt to scare you out of it by means of a different set of attacks. Consequently, some who are excited about the Christ life get discouraged because it seems things aren't going right. But there is no need to fear.

The conquest of Canaan pictures the Spirit-filled life. It is the "Promised Land." In the Old Testament the Canaanites were defeated by the sure word of promise to God's people. But they did not just lay down their arms. They fought the inevitable as the children of Israel advanced. Similarly, Satan was defeated by the mighty "It is finished!" But though disarmed at the cross, he and his cohorts of evil fight every inch of the way through their various tactics of deception. However, just as the Promised Land was taken by faith, so you too may "Submit yourselves therefore to God. Resist the devil, and he will flee from you" (James 4:7).

This is the provision of divine authority to be victorious in the spiritual realm. As you may access by faith Christ's divine ability to counteract and overcome the world and the flesh in the physical realm, so you may access by faith Christ's divine authority to counterattack and overrule the devil and his evil forces in the spiritual realm.

When you yield to your flesh, you place yourself *under* a defeated foe (Gen. 3:15; John 16:11; 12:31–32; Col. 2:14–15; Heb. 2:14). But when you walk in the Spirit, you may also claim your authority in Christ at the throne to *overrule* the enemy. Remember that in the spiritual realm, Satan is at a disadvantage—because he is thoroughly defeated.

Temptation through Combined Causes

Sometimes temptation

approaches through the physical realm and the spiritual realm simultaneously. You are dealing with both an apparent cause and a non-apparent cause in conjunction with each other. You might say they are "direct-indirect attacks."

In this case evil spirits in the spiritual realm may target a worldly or fleshly snare in the physical realm at a particular individual. Satan and his evil cohorts despise a believer who learns how to exercise authority over them. Therefore, at times they may focus on you in an attempt to pull you down from your position of faith in Christ at the throne. But since we are not ignorant of Satan's devices, there is no need for evil forces to succeed. Learn to recognize temptation that approaches through combined causes.

Since Satan is a defeated foe, his major tactic is deception. These deceptions are "the wiles of the devil" (Eph. 6:11). But as just noted, we "are not ignorant of his devices" (2 Cor. 2:11).

Distortion is a deception that involves both the physical and spiritual realms. Perhaps someone makes an offensive comment to you or does something that is offensive to you. In reality it is a minor matter, a mere "bump in the road," and is only in the physical realm. Yet the offense may be magnified in your perception until it appears to be mountain-sized. This distortion comes from the spiritual realm.

If you do not recognize this as a spiritual attack and access God's grace, you may respond with a fury that matches a mountain-sized offense, and the offender will wonder, "What's the matter with you?" This type of distortion undoubtedly is involved in many church tensions and even church splits.

Distortion involves excessiveness, which you must learn to recognize as a trick of the enemy. Perhaps you are at the store, and there is an inordinate attraction to buy a particular item. Recognize the excessive element to the attraction, and reject it.

As impulsiveness reveals the flesh, so compulsiveness reveals satanic involvement.

Perhaps you are in a crowd of people in a store, at work or even in church, and you are drawn inordinately toward someone of the opposite gender. Recognize the excessive attraction as distortion, and reject it. What's amazing in this kind of scenario is that, after the attack is over, you may realize that the person isn't even attractive!

Excessive distraction is another deception that involves both the physical and spiritual realms. Soon after the Lord taught me these very truths, I was scheduled to leave on a trip to Asia and needed to do a lot of preparation. The day before the trip I went to get a haircut and took some Bible study books with me so I could finish preparing as I waited my turn for the barber's chair.

The barbershop had a TV on, and on previous visits it was usually tuned to something like a fishing program or a ballgame. But this time, when I shifted my weight as I studied, I was confronted with indecent images on the screen. Quickly I took the Lord's purity and with liberty went back to my work. But forgetting my setting and engrossed in my study, I again shifted my position and was confronted with filth. This occurred several more times, and though I took the Lord's purity each time and was freed to do right, it was obviously a major distraction.

Then it occurred to me that this excessive distraction might involve a satanic attack to keep me from needed study. Certainly there was an apparent cause—the television content. But I wondered if a non-apparent cause was also involved. So in my heart I claimed my position in Christ at the throne and exercised His authority over any satanic involvement in the situation. Immediately the barber, who was calmly using a shaver on the back of a man's head, began to tremble. He pulled the shaver away and set it on the counter, reached for the remote control and changed the programming to something decent. I wanted to shout "Hallelujah!" What a glorious provision the Lord has given the saints!

Once while preaching this very truth in a new church in Ireland, a mother took her crying baby out during the invitation time at the closing of a service. But the distraction continued because of the small facility we were in. When I recognized the potential of distraction from the enemy, I—and unknown to me, the mother as well—claimed Christ's provision over the enemy. Immediately the baby became calm and quiet.

Deliverance from Combined-Cause Temptation

The combination of "Christ in you" (Gal. 2:20) and "you in Christ" (Eph. 1–2, 6) form the foundation of faith for temptation that approaches through combined causes. Simply appropriate Christ's divine ability to counteract and overcome the world and the flesh and appropriate Christ's divine authority to counterattack and overrule the powers of darkness. Just transact with the Lord, "I claim Christ in me and I in Christ," and the Faithful One will meet the need. What a comprehensive provision for victory in both the physical and spiritual realms!

Qualifying Principles

Along with the customized provision referred to in First Corinthians 10:13 and expanded through other passages, our text also delineates several qualifying principles.

The Way of Escape is Time-Sensitive

The text plainly says, "There hath no temptation taken you but such as is common to man: but God is faithful, who will not suffer [allow] you to be tempted above [beyond] that ye are able." But have you ever felt tempted beyond what you are able?

Has temptation ever seemed overwhelming? Has it ever seemed like you really didn't even have a choice? Why does our experience seem to defy what the text affirms?

The answer lies in discovering the point of the promise found in the last part of the text: "but will with the temptation also make [the] way to escape, that ye may be able to bear it." When does God promise the way of escape? The text specifies "with [together with] the temptation." This detail implies the crisis moment is when the temptation first approaches. It is then you have the window of opportunity to take the way of escape. It is time sensitive. If you do not take the escape ramp provided on the curve of temptation, you will pass it up.

Suppose temptation confronts you, and you immediately sense the pull of the flesh one way and the leadership of the Spirit another. If you are not careful to take the way of escape immediately, you may begin to entertain the possibility of the temptation and, in a few fleeting moments, begin to follow after the temptation. If you do so, you just embraced the temptation in your heart—and missed the way of escape. But since you have not committed the outward act of sin, there may still be a battle. This is when the temptation will seem overwhelming and seem like you don't have a choice. It's because when you did have a choice, you made the *wrong* choice.

Imagine a new convert who decides to give up his habit of smoking and discards all his cigarettes. Things seem to go well for two weeks. Then one day, as he drives home from work, he sees a new advertisement on a billboard—the very brand of cigarettes he smoked just two weeks before. Immediately the temptation to smoke confronts him.

Remember, being tempted is not sin. Jesus said, "Pray that ye enter not into temptation" (Luke 22:40). Therefore, *entering into* temptation is sin but being tempted is not. This is a wonderful truth to realize, since temptation is often out of our control.

This new convert is being tempted to smoke. That temptation is not sin. Then perhaps he looks down the street in front of him and sees a store—one of the places where he used to buy cigarettes, before he quit. Tragically, he drives to that store with the intent of buying some cigarettes. As he pulls into the parking lot, has he smoked yet? No. But has he passed the point of the promise for the way of escape? Yes. In his heart he has already embraced the sin. That is why, while still sitting in the parking lot, the temptation will seem beyond his choice—because when he did have a choice, he made the wrong one! His only hope at that point is to come clean with God (1 John 1:9), which is a corrective provision.

The lesson ought to be obvious. Since the way of escape is time-sensitive, learn to take the way of escape immediately.

The Way of Escape is Preventative

The fact that the Scripture uses the word "escape" implies that the way of escape is a matter of prevention, not correction. It is a matter of deliverance, not confession. You need confession only when you enter into the temptation in heart or act. Confession is for cleansing when you fail to take the way of escape.

When temptation faces you, but you have not yet entered into the temptation, confession actually enters the temptation by "owning" it. It essentially says, "That's me; therefore, I confess." But you must remember that being tempted is not sin. So it is not you. If you confess before you have actually entered the temptation, it brings about a binding effect instead of a release.

The way of escape is a matter of rejecting the temptation, not accepting it through confession. Whether approaching from the world, the flesh or the devil, you must reject temptation based on Christ's provision. You must say, "That's not me. I refuse that based on the provision of Christ in me and/or me in Christ."

When a fiery dart is hurled at you, is that you? Obviously, it is not. To experience the way of escape, simply reject the fiery dart based on your position in Christ. When a worldly snare grabs your attention, is that you? Again, the answer is obvious. So reject the snare based on the indwelling Christ. But what about when your flesh responds to some trigger of temptation, and you physiologically feel the pull in your flesh toward the temptation, is that you? I used to think so, and it was the cause of confessing and owning temptations, instead of rejecting and disowning them.

We must remember that through our death with Christ, we were severed from indwelling sin, and through our resurrection with Christ, we are united to the indwelling Christ. Therefore, that "pull" in our flesh is not us! That is why Paul said, "It is no more I that do it, but sin that dwelleth in me" (Rom. 7:17, 20). If we yield to the flesh, we take on responsibility, but initially that pull is not us. Therefore, reject that fleshly feel based on your death and resurrection with Christ. Immediately the "pull" will disappear as you experience the liberating way of escape.

When preaching in my younger years, I remember times when the Spirit of God moved me, and a flow of words proceeded out of my mouth that was not in my notes. The flow of words often ended in a dramatic pause. In this pause the thought would roll across my mind, "Hey! That was pretty good! You did a great job!" Not recognizing the temptation to pride was not me, in my heart I would confess the pride instead of taking the way of escape. Inevitably, I would lose something in the preaching, and the service would be hindered. What I needed to do was simply say, "I reject that. That's not me," and continue on in freedom.

Perhaps you truly deal scripturally with some bitterness issue. Then a few weeks later, that old thought process of bitterness comes rolling through your mind. If you say, "Oh God, how could this bitterness still be with me? Please forgive me," you will spiral downward. Rather, you can say, "That's not me. I already dealt with that. Therefore, I reject this attack based on my provision in Christ," and experience continued freedom.

Before I understood this truth, I would confess and confess all day long. By the end of the day I was pummeled. How liberating it is to know the way of escape is preventative.

The Way of Escape is Trustworthy

The text says, "God is faithful" to provide the way of escape with each temptation. In very fact, the way of escape is a person. Jesus said, "I am the way" (John 14:6). He is the way of truth for life. The way of escape is trustworthy, because He is the trustworthy One. He is *always* trustworthy in His availability as well as in His dependability. Jesus is greater than this wicked world, our sinful flesh and the deceitful serpent, for "greater is he that is in you, than he that is in the world" (1 John 4:4). Since you were born again, Jesus was available every time you were tempted to deliver you from whatever you faced. There is no case for excusing yourself because of your background, bad character and so forth. But the good news is Jesus will always be there as the way of escape every time you are tempted. Take Jesus—the unfailing deliverer!

On several occasions over the years of travel across America from coast to coast, we have seen a truck on an escape ramp— life preserved and cargo spared—because the driver took the way of escape. Learn to always take the way of escape and experience the overcoming life! The overcoming life opens the channel for the overflowing life.

• • • • •

Questions for Personal Reflection

1. What situations came to mind where the appropriate truth was not applied to a particular approach of temptation?

2. What scenarios came to mind regarding the need to take the way of escape immediately, since it is time-sensitive?

3. What temptations have you been confessing instead of rejecting?

7

THE OVERFLOWING LIFE
How to Impact Others with the Life of Christ

In the last day, that great day of the feast, Jesus stood and cried, saying, If any man thirst, let him come unto me, and drink. He that believeth on me, as the scripture hath said, out of his belly shall flow rivers of living water. (But this spake he of the Spirit, which they that believe on him should receive: for the Holy Ghost was not yet given; because that Jesus was not yet glorified.) JOHN 7:37–39

IN the late 1970s my father took me on one of his trips to the Bible lands. We began in Egypt. As a fifteen-year-old, I marveled at seeing sights similar to what Moses might have seen, such as the ancient pyramids, which date back not mere centuries but millennia. At the museum in Cairo, the tour guide led the way through the general exhibits of ancient artifacts, but my father took me aside privately to another part of the museum.

Paying extra, we entered a room that housed the mummies of the Egyptian Pharaohs. They were displayed horizontally in encased glass—some with their faces uncovered, others their feet as well. We viewed Ramses II, Thutmoses III and others. As a student of history, my father pointed out the mummy he concluded was the Pharaoh of the Exodus, the stiff-necked ruler who hardened his heart. I stood amazed to actually look at his face (and by the way, his neck was still stiff!).

Then we made our way across the Sinai Peninsula. The tour bus stopped in the desert at what looked like a pile of rocks. But one rock was split, and out of the divide gushed forth water. Could this natural spring be the result of one of the wilderness miracles, when God brought forth water out of the smitten rock? We all drank from the overflow of this fresh, pure stream.

First Corinthians 10:4 explains that the children of Israel "did all drink the same spiritual drink: for they drank of that spiritual Rock that followed them: and that Rock was Christ." The physical pictures the spiritual. Moses was to strike the rock only once because Christ died once for all.

In John 7 the Jews celebrated the Feast of Tabernacles (or tents), remembering the time of God's provision in the wilderness. The week-long feast included ceremonies involving water, commemorating the Lord's provision of water in the wilderness. With this imagery before the people's minds, Jesus stood up and cried out, "If any man thirst, let him come unto me, and drink. He that believeth on me, as the scripture hath said, out of his belly shall flow rivers of living water."

What a beautiful picture of the Spirit-filled life for service! There is a difference of purpose between the Spirit-filled life for holiness and the Spirit-filled life for service. Holiness is *being* right, or personal victory. Service is *doing* right, or ministry to others. Holiness accesses Christ's life *to you*. Service accesses Christ's life through you *to others*. As the filling for holiness provides for personal victory, so the overflowing for service provides for effective ministry. In order to impact others effectively, Christ must flow through us to them.

Effective ministry may also involve accessing Christ's authority to deal with the powers of darkness that hinder others from seeing the glorious light of the gospel of Christ. We addressed the provision and access of throne seat authority in chapter four.

Jesus asserts that, through dependence on Him, from your innermost being "shall flow rivers of living water." The purpose of this promise is not to receive eternal life as in John 3:16, but to access the abundant life for others. The overflowing life impacts others with the life of Christ. Since drinking at the fountain of Christ accesses the overflowing life for service, we must regularly drink afresh of the fullness of Christ. But practically, what is involved in such imagery? Notice three features.

The Prerequisite of the Overflowing Life

Jesus says, "If any man thirst." The conditional "if" reveals some are unaware of their need. The descriptive word "thirst" uses the present tense, indicating continual thirst: "if anyone is thirsty." The key thought is to *know your need continually* for the supernatural dynamic of the overflowing life. Know your need when you feel it and when you don't. Certainly God allows us at times to feel our need. Yet there are other times when we may not feel it, but we are still just as much in need. If you do not know your need continually, you are self-dependent.

Self-dependence for personal victory leads to defeat—the obvious defeat of reigning sin or the subtle defeat of self-righteous rags. Self-dependence for effective service also leads to defeat—the obvious defeat of failure *to minister* to others or the subtle defeat of failure *in ministry* to others. Tragically, when speaking of gospel witness, many Christians simply ignore this responsibility. Others resolve to obey the Great Commission but make the mistake of witness dependent on the flesh. This leads to frustration and failure. Many who begin with fresh resolve to witness regularly eventually cease, even though their resolve may last a few years. Evidently, the flesh can take only so much. The sheer duty of going through ministry motions with no carrying power is not productive. This ineffectiveness causes many to drop out of the race. It is better to let the revealed need draw you back to the fountain of Christ.

My father said that as a young man, he could not preach two good sermons in a row. If he preached a "dud," he would seek the Lord for the next service. This faith accessed grace, and God blessed. Then he would think, "Well, I'm finally getting there," and he would not really cast himself upon the Lord for the next sermon and so would inevitably fail. Eventually, he learned to know his need for the supernatural dynamic continually.

In the fall of 2000, we held a Netcasters Evangelism Training Seminar (NETSeminar) in Singapore. The course teaches the Spirit-filled life for evangelistic witness. A dear lady, whom someone described as being merely "in the woodwork of the church," came to the seminar because she knew her need. God graciously opened her eyes to life-changing truth. Soon she evidenced the overflowing life and became such an effective witness for Christ she later served as a trainer in NETSeminars.

Another man, who had not led a soul to Christ for twenty years, also attended that particular NETSeminar in Singapore. Soon he accessed and evidenced the overflowing life. During the next year, in high-tech, wealthy, professional Singapore, the Lord used him to lead 200 souls to Christ. The overflowing life of Jesus is effective!

Know your need continually, so that you might find the answer to your need.

The Principle of the Overflowing Life

For those who recognize their need, Jesus invites, "Let him come . . . and drink. He that believeth . . ." All the verbs are in the present tense indicating continuous action. The key thought is to *depend on Jesus repeatedly* for His divine work through you.

The Imagery

Christ pictures Himself as the cleft rock from which the water of life flows. He is the spring of living water. Christ is the inexhaustible fountain, and so He invites the thirsty to keep coming and keep drinking of His never-ending supply. In fact, the two verbs in the phrase "let him come unto me and drink" are in the imperative mood. In love, Christ not only offers but commands us to avail ourselves of Him as the fountain of living water. This is more than an invitation; it is an obligation.

The Issue

The issue behind the imagery of coming and drinking at the fountain is "He that believeth on me," or literally, "he who keeps depending on Me." When you avail yourself of this offer repeatedly, you develop the habit of faith. The focus is on the object of faith, emphasized in the word "me," referring to Christ. Depend regularly on Christ's leadership by surrendering to His will. Also, depend regularly on Christ's enabling power by surrendering to His strength. This is the "give all" and "take all" discussed in chapter five. Both are vital to fulfilling the scriptural principle of "he that believeth on me."

A lady in Ireland came to embrace the Spirit-filled life for holiness. As a result, she began to exercise faith and access grace for personal victory. Then the Spirit awakened her to the potential of the Spirit-filled life for service. At that point she had never led a soul to Christ. She promised the Lord she would obey His next prompting to declare Christ. This implies the Spirit had prompted her before. Her surrender to obey the Spirit's next prompting revealed dependence on Christ's leadership.

The following day the Spirit prompted her to speak to a young lady. She wrote my wife and me about this, testifying that at the moment the Spirit prompted her to speak, she was terrified. But thankfully, faith is not a feeling. Remembering her surrender to obey but feeling her own weakness, she called on the Lord for divine intervention and began to speak. Her surrender to trust in the Spirit's power revealed dependence on Christ's enabling.

She further testified that when she trusted to obey by opening her mouth, it was as if the Holy Spirit took over. The Lord granted a thorough witness, followed by another witness the next day, resulting in the young girl calling upon the name of the Lord. Over the years that first soul has been followed by many others because this lady learned to depend on both Christ's purpose and power in the matter of service.

Notice as she physically interacted by faith, the Spirit spiritually intervened in grace, freeing her to speak and the young lady to understand. Without the step of faith this dynamic would have been missed. This is not a matter of going into a spiritual phone booth and coming out a "super soul winner," but trusting (even with trembling) to obey and the Spirit of God meeting you in the moment of the step of faith.

Depend on Jesus repeatedly, so that you might experience His life.

The Promise of the Overflowing Life

Following the invitation to drink at the fountain, Jesus promises, "as the scripture hath said, out of his belly shall flow rivers of living water. (But this spake he of the Spirit, which they that believe on him should receive: for the Holy Ghost was not yet given; because that Jesus was not yet glorified.)"

The key thought here is to *experience Christ's life abundantly* for others.

The Source

The phrase "out of his belly" literally means out of his heart or innermost being. This references the union between the regenerated spirit and the Holy Spirit. The Holy Spirit imparts the life of Christ through the human spirit, through the human soul, through the human body, out to others. This is not only *Christ* imparted *to you*; it is *Christ* imparted through you *to others*. From the fountain to the filling to the overflowing—the overflowing life originates with the fountain. Christ is the source of all life.

The Purpose

The phrase "shall flow rivers of living water" shapes the purpose of accessing the overflowing life. First, Jesus desires us to be *channels*. The wording "shall flow" highlights this as a biblical reality, not merely a poetic nicety. A channel allows the source of supply to reach the need of that supply.

My family and I travel in a RV in revival work. When I arrive at a church, I connect a water hose to a water spigot and then to the trailer. The key is not the hose but the source of water. Yet you need a channel to get the water to the RV. Likewise, we are channels of the life of Jesus to those in need. The key is not the channel but Jesus, the source of supply. Yet God has chosen to use us as channels to bring the water of life to those in need.

Second, we are to be channels of *abundance*. The word "rivers" reveals God's ample supply. Once I was taken to see a large spring that bubbled up to fill a deep pond of clear water and spilled out into a river. Yet Jesus said "rivers," not just one but many. Is this not a picture of abundance?

Facts and Promises

Facts are in the present tense or refer to past events with present ramifications. Promises are in the future tense, either by being stated as such explicitly or by being implied as such because of a condition that must first be met. Facts refer to that which *is*. Promises refer to that which *will be*. Facts represent *realities*. Promises represent "potentialities." . . .

Facts are the provision for your immediate or present need. Promises are the provision for your coming or future need. Facts form the foundation of faith for your present experience. Promises form the foundation of faith for your future experience.[20]

Third, the total purpose is to be channels of abundance *of life*. The specific wording "of living water" emphasizes this thought in the word "living," which is a verb form of the noun *life* found in the phrase "eternal life." Jesus is *the Christian life*. He is "that eternal life" (1 John 1:2). This is the life that people desperately need.

Just as water from the snow-covered mountains, when channeled down into the San Joaquin Valley in California, turned a desert into one of the greatest agricultural centers of the world, so the water of life, when channeled into the valley of souls, turns a desert into a fruitful field.

The Emphasis

Verse 39 explains, "But this spake he of the Spirit, which they that believe on him should receive: for the Holy Ghost was not yet given; because that Jesus was not yet glorified." Jesus made this statement before Pentecost, but at Pentecost the Spirit was sent. The first phrase "the Spirit" incorporates the definite article *the*, emphasizing the person of the Spirit. However, the second phrase "the Holy Ghost [Spirit]" leaves out the definite article. Obviously, the translation uses the definite article in the English rendering to avoid awkwardness, but actually the definite article is absent. This emphasizes the quality of the Spirit or "Holy Spirit-ness." The emphasis of the promise of rivers of living water flowing through you as the channel is the quality of the Spirit attending your ministry. This is the supernatural dynamic necessary for effective ministry.

Would it not make a difference if the quality of Jesus attended our words in ministry? Certainly the ministry that ought to take place within the home between husband and wife and also in child-training could and would be greatly enhanced if the quality of Jesus carried the words. Also, ministry within the local church would be greatly blessed and effective if *Holy Spirit-ness* energized the communication of truth.

Ultimately, it is the quality of Jesus that makes gospel witness powerful, freeing us to speak and freeing our hearers to hear with understanding. When this is the case, as you declare the message of good news, people are literally confronted in the spiritual realm with the Savior of the message! This is the overflowing life—the life of Jesus flowing out to others!

Know your need continually for the supernatural dynamic of the overflowing life. Depend on Jesus repeatedly for His divine work through you. Then experience Christ's life abundantly for others.

Simplified Steps to Accessing the Overflowing Life

What are the specific steps of dependence on Jesus for the overflowing life? The provision for holiness or personal victory is based on facts or what *is*, and is accessible by simply *taking* the reality of the facts and *acting* upon it. However, the provision for service or effective ministry is based on promises or what *will be*, and is accessible primarily through the additional step of *ask-*

ing for the potentiality of the promises, then *taking* as the Lord gives, and finally *acting* upon it.

Since the promise of power for service—Christ through you to others—is given in the future tense as seen in the phrase "shall flow," the first step is to *ask* for the quality of the Spirit. Ask the Spirit to free you to speak. Ask the Spirit to free those to whom you minister to hear with understanding. Simply ask for the quality of the Spirit to inundate the whole ministry process. When you ask in faith, the Lord gives according to the promise pleaded and bears witness with your spirit, "You have your request." Then you must *take* what has been given and *act* on it by speaking the truth. These steps comprise "He that believeth on me."

Luke 11:13 gives a similar promise. "If ye then, being evil, know how to give good gifts unto your children: how much more shall your heavenly Father give the Holy Spirit [literally, "Holy Spirit-ness" or the quality of the Holy Spirit] to them that ask him?" The first step is literally spelled out: "ask." Since Jesus promises that the Father "shall . . . give" to those who ask for the quality of the Spirit, then as you ask for the Spirit's ministry, at some point the Spirit will bear witness with your spirit that you have your request, perhaps even through speaking the words of the promise to your heart, indicating you have been given that for which you asked. At that point, just *take* the provision as a definite transaction, and say thank you. Then you can, with divine enabling, *act* upon it as you declare the good news of Jesus Christ.

To act without asking and taking would be self-dependent acting. But to act after you have asked and received is God-dependent, Spirit-enabled acting. This is the overflowing life for effective service.

Quite frankly, it is as simple as John 3:16. In fact, the condition is the same—believing on Jesus. Only the purpose varies. In John 3:16 the purpose of believing is to receive the eternal life of Jesus yourself. In John 7:37–39 the purpose is to access the abundant life of Jesus in you for others. Just as you can be saved and know it, based on the sure words of God, and have a clean heart and know it, based on the sure words of God, and have a filled life for holiness and know it, based on the sure words of God, so you can have an overflowing life for service and know it, based on the sure words of God. You can be filled with the Spirit and know it because the Bible says so! God's Word is true, regardless of your feelings at a particular moment.

For years I acted without asking and taking, and I was frustrated and defeated in service. As the Spirit brought me along the revival road for cleansing and victory, He also awakened me to the overflowing life. So I began to ask. But not yet understanding the importance of a definite taking, I would then act (witness, etc.) wondering and hoping God would undertake. But when you merely "hope" you are Spirit-filled, you are lacking the definite step of taking.

At that time while preaching at a conference, a lady told me she would ask for the Spirit to fill her. Then she queried, "How do I know if He is?" Well, that's what I was often wondering myself! But the Holy Spirit, gracious to both of us, gave me the right answer. I explained that like salvation, when you call on the name of the Lord, you can take God at His word that you will be saved, so also when you ask for the Spirit's power in service, you can take God at His word that you will be empowered. I emphasized, "Just *take* God at His word regardless of how you feel." She brightened as the Spirit nurtured faith in her heart based on truth, and went away rejoicing.

Later I thought to myself, *That was good advice! That's what I need to do!* Although I had been aware of the concept and had even articulated the essential truth in sermons, that day the Spirit fully convinced me of what I had only known marginally, and it has been life-changing!

A young evangelist who worked hard to lead people to Christ came to understand the Spirit-filled life for holiness and service in a definite way. He testified that prior to that point he saw about fifteen souls profess Christ each year. After that point he saw sixty souls profess Christ in the first three months. Now he sees several hundred profess Christ each year. What a glorious difference the overflowing life of Jesus makes!

The difference is not the channel by itself. The difference is a channel cleansed, filled and overflowing with the life of Jesus. Simply *ask*, *take* and *act*—and watch God work. Since drinking at the fountain of Christ accesses the overflowing life for service, we must regularly drink afresh of the fullness of Jesus Christ.

· · · · ·

Questions for Personal Reflection

1. How have you demonstrated self-dependence, and therefore, the need to continually thirst for the Fountain?

2. In what ways have you observed the supernatural dynamic of the life of Jesus flowing through you to impact others?

3. Which step or steps of faith seem to be lacking in your practice: ask, take or act?

8

THE WHOLE PACKAGE
The Baptism of the Holy Spirit

For ye are all the children of God by faith in Christ Jesus. For as many of you as have been baptized into Christ have put on Christ. GALATIANS 3:26–27

A FULL biblical perspective regarding the baptism of the Holy Spirit ignites theology. Theology on fire means the people of God on fire. But the mere mention of "the baptism of the Holy Spirit" in a modern context evokes a variety of ideas and emotions. During my ordination council in 1987, someone asked, "What is the baptism of the Holy Spirit?" At that time I answered in the vein of John R. Rice, for whom I was named. In the following moments there was "no small stir" among the preachers over the meaning of "the baptism of the Holy Spirit."

Plainly, many disagree over the meaning of this subject. In some cases the disagreement is a matter of semantics. Over the years this has caused me to seek to be more precise in my terminology. Certainly, it is fair to argue for particular terms. However, some become argumentative, and some even urge separation from those who do not use their choice of terms. Yet most agree there is Holy Spirit power available by faith in order to fulfill all that God has for us. This is the main point and is the desperate need of the hour!

D.L. Moody and R.A. Torrey emphasized the baptism of the Holy Spirit as a baptism of power accessible by faith. Since many believers are sadly anemic in both their life and service, this concept leads believers to seek this "baptism of power." It is worth noting that both Moody and Torrey evidenced the power of the Holy Spirit in their ministries.

However, the average theological textbook less than a century later emphasized the baptism of the Holy Spirit as something that takes place at the moment of salvation, never to be sought after again. The proof text given is usually First Corinthians 12:13: "For by one Spirit are we all baptized into one body."

Is the baptism of the Holy Spirit something believers need to seek, or is it something believers possess already? Or is there an element of truth in both emphases that you must embrace to be biblically balanced? What is the full perspective?

One-sided truth becomes off balance. The doctrine of Christ has two emphases: He is very God and very man. The doctrine of the Trinity also has two emphases: God is one God in three persons. You must embrace both emphases, or you will end up in doctrinal disarray. In the same way, the baptism of the Holy Spirit has two emphases that you must embrace to be biblically balanced.

Because of the debate which surrounds the phrase *the baptism of the Holy Spirit*, I will be a little more technical in this chapter than in the other chapters of this book. But I will also seek to summarize the conclusions simply at the end of each section.

The baptism of the Holy Spirit addresses the whole package of both the provision and accessibility of Christ's life. A careful examination of every occurrence of Spirit baptism in the New

Testament reveals the baptism of the Holy Spirit is one baptism with two directions, representing two provisions accessible by faith in order to be functional. Since the baptism of the Holy Spirit is both a glorious reality and a provisional potential for every believer, believers must depend upon the facts and access the function of the baptism of the Holy Spirit by faith.

The Facts

You may discover the facts of the baptism of the Holy Spirit by examining both the explicit usages of the terms for baptism in the contexts of Spirit baptism and the implicit ramifications through the analogy of faith that compares Scripture with Scripture. Many focus on the Spirit baptizing believers *into* Christ but fail to account for the contexts where Christ baptizes believers *with* the Spirit or vice versa. But before investigating this we must briefly address the subject of water baptism and Spirit baptism.

Some debate whether certain passages refer to water baptism or Spirit baptism. Two questions can aid in this quandary: *Who* is doing the baptizing—deity or a human? And what is the element being baptized *into* or *with*—deity or water? When a human is specifically named as the one doing the baptizing, like in the story of Philip and the Ethiopian Eunuch (Acts 8:38), or when water is specifically named as the element being baptized into, as indicated in the Eunuch's question, "See, here is water; what doth hinder me to be baptized?" (Acts 8:36), then the reference is to water baptism. However, when deity does the baptizing, which in the New Testament will be either Christ or the Spirit, rather than a human, or when deity is named as the element being baptized into or with, which again in the New Testament will be either Christ or the Spirit, then the context is Spirit baptism and not water baptism. The inspired word choices solve the quandary. Although water baptism is not the focus of this study, water baptism beautifully pictures Spirit baptism, as John the Baptist indicates in his analogy, "I indeed have baptized you with water: but he shall baptize you with the Holy Ghost" (Mark 1:8).

One Baptism: Two Directions

Since water baptism illustrates Spirit baptism and Spirit baptism explains the significance of water baptism, Ephesians 4:5 may properly speak of "one baptism." Yet the baptism of the Holy Spirit includes two directions revolving around the words "into" and "with." When someone trusts Christ as Savior, the Holy Spirit baptizes the believer *into* Christ, while simultaneously Christ baptizes the believer *with* the Holy Spirit. When a sponge is immersed *into* water, the sponge is also inundated *with* the water, as the water immediately moves into the sponge. So also when a believer is immersed *into* Christ, the believer is also inundated *with* the Spirit, as the Spirit immediately moves into the believer.

By the Spirit into Christ: The first direction of Spirit baptism is when the Holy Spirit immerses the believer *into* Christ. This direction of Spirit baptism is revealed in four New Testament contexts. The verb "baptize" (*baptizo*) occurs with the preposition "into" (*eis*) four times in three contexts (1 Cor. 12:13; Gal. 3:27; Rom. 6:3 [twice]) and the noun "baptism" (*baptisma*) occurs with the preposition "into" (*eis*) once in one of the verb contexts (Rom. 6:4) and once in an additional context that implies the concept of "into" (Col. 2:12). Each of the four contexts provides significant details to the first direction of Spirit baptism.

1. First Corinthians 12:12–13 reveals the agent who baptizes, the ones being baptized and the element into which they are baptized: "For as the body is one, and hath many members . . . so also is Christ. For by one Spirit are we all baptized into one body." The agent who baptizes is the Holy Spirit ("by one

Spirit"). This detail is unique to First Corinthians 12:13. The ones being baptized are believers ("we" refers back to 12:1, where Paul calls his readers "brethren"). The element into which believers are baptized is the body of Christ ("Christ . . . one body"). This context emphasizes the agency of the Spirit and teaches that the Holy Spirit baptizes believers into the body of Christ.

2. Galatians 3:26–27 reveals the ones being baptized, the means, the timing and the element of this direction of Spirit baptism: "For ye are all the children of God by faith in Christ Jesus. For as many of you as have been baptized into Christ have put on Christ." Again, the ones being baptized are believers ("the children of God"). The means of the baptism is faith ("by faith in Christ Jesus"). The timing of the baptism is the moment of faith for salvation ("faith [referring back to 3:24—"justified by faith"] . . . For as many of you as have been baptized"). The past tense refers to the transaction of saving faith. The element into which believers are baptized is Christ ("into Christ"). This context emphasizes the timing of Spirit baptism and teaches that believers are baptized into Christ when they believe in Jesus for salvation.

3. Romans 6:3–5 reveals the ones being baptized and the element into which they are baptized. It also states the significance of being baptized into that element:

> Know ye not, that so many of us as were baptized into Jesus Christ were baptized into his death? Therefore we are buried with him by baptism into death: that like as Christ was raised up from the dead by the glory of the Father, even so we also should walk in newness of life. For if we have been planted together in the likeness of his death, we shall be also in the likeness of his resurrection.

Once again, the ones being baptized are believers ("us," referring back to 6:2—"we, that are dead to sin"). The element into which believers are baptized is Christ ("into Jesus Christ"). However, this context also reveals that in being "baptized into Jesus Christ" believers are therefore "baptized into his death" and "his resurrection." The logic is clear. If believers "have been planted together," the wording of which pictures being baptized or placed into "the likeness of his death," then believers must of necessity be united together as well "in the likeness of his resurrection."

These are tremendous identification truths. Baptism into Christ necessitates the fact or reality of being identified in Christ's death and resurrection. The purpose is also stated: "that like as Christ was raised up from the dead . . . even so we also should walk in newness of life." This context emphasizes the significance of baptism into Christ and teaches that when believers are baptized into Christ, they are baptized into His death and resurrection.

4. Colossians 2:12 reveals the ones being baptized, the means, the timing and the significance of baptism into Christ: "buried with him in baptism, wherein also ye are risen with him through the faith of the operation of God, who hath raised him from the dead." The ones being baptized are believers ("ye," referring back to 2:6—"ye . . . received Christ"). The means of the baptism is faith ("through . . . faith"). The timing of the baptism is the moment of faith for salvation, since the past tense of the verbs refers to the transaction of faith. The element into which believers are baptized is implied as being Christ, since the significance of this implication is indicated in the words "buried with him in baptism" and "risen with him." Like Romans 6, this context emphasizes the significance of baptism into Christ and teaches that believers are buried with Christ and raised with Christ.

In summary, the first direction of Spirit baptism is being baptized by the Spirit *into* Christ. The agent who baptizes is the Spirit, the ones being baptized are believers, the element into which believers are baptized is Christ, the means of the baptism is faith, the timing of the baptism is the transaction of faith for salvation, and the significance of this direction of Spirit baptism is that believers are identified with Christ in His death and resurrection. Union with Christ in His resurrection life introduces the second direction of Spirit baptism.[21]

By the Son with the Spirit: The second direction of Spirit baptism is when Christ invests the believer *with* the Holy Spirit. This direction of Spirit baptism is revealed in six New Testament contexts explicitly and in two others implicitly. The verb "baptize" (*baptizo*) occurs with the preposition "with" (*en*) in six contexts (Matt. 3:11; Mark 1:8; Luke 3:16; John 1:33; Acts 1:5, 11:16) and with the concept of "with" in two contexts (1 Cor. 12:13; Gal. 3:27). The explicit and implicit contexts provide significant details to the second direction of Spirit baptism.[21]

1. The explicit passages may be categorized according to their grammatical emphasis. Matthew 3:11, Mark 1:8 and Luke 3:16 all reveal the agent who baptizes in this direction of Spirit baptism, the ones being baptized and the description of what they are being baptized with. In all three passages John the Baptist says of Jesus that "he shall baptize you with the Holy Ghost." Matthew and Luke add "and with fire." The agent who baptizes is Jesus Christ ("he"). The ones being baptized are believers ("you"). The description of what believers are baptized with is the power of the Holy Spirit ("with [the] Holy Ghost and with fire"). The key to understanding this aspect is noting that in the Greek the definite article "the" is actually absent before the name "Holy Ghost." Grammatically, this places the emphasis on the quality of the person named. This emphasis on the quality of "Holy Spirit-ness" focuses on the Spirit's operation and ministry, which is essentially His power. These three contexts emphasize Christ as the one doing the baptizing and teach Christ baptizes believers with the power of the Holy Spirit.

John 1:33 also reveals the agent who baptizes in this direction of Spirit baptism and the description of what the agent baptizes with. But instead of naming the ones being baptized, it simply focuses on the baptizing. John the Baptist says that Jesus is "he which baptizeth with the Holy Ghost." The agent who baptizes is Jesus ("he"). The description of what Jesus baptizes with is the power of the Holy Spirit ("with [the] Holy Ghost"). Again the definite article "the" is actually absent, placing the emphasis on the quality of the person named. Also, the focus is on the baptizing ("which baptizeth"). John's account does not use the future tense, as do the Synoptics ("shall baptize"), but the present tense, indicating that Jesus is the one who *is baptizing*. This grammatical point implies that the baptizing refers to more than the Day of Pentecost, which is of great significance. Like the Synoptic passages, this context also emphasizes Christ as the one doing the baptizing and teaches that Christ is baptizing believers with the power of the Holy Spirit.

Acts 1:5 and 11:16 both reveal the ones being baptized, the description of what they are being baptized with, and the context reveals the timing of the baptism. In Acts 1:5 Jesus said, "For John truly baptized with water; but ye shall be baptized with the Holy Ghost not many days hence." In Acts 11:16 Peter quoted the Lord as saying, "John indeed baptized with water; but ye shall be baptized with the Holy Ghost." The ones being baptized are believers ("ye" is identified in the next verse as "us, who believed on the Lord Jesus Christ"). The description of what believers are baptized with is the power of the Holy Spirit ("with [the] Holy Ghost"). Again the absence of the definite article emphasizes "Holy Spirit-ness." The timing of being baptized with the Holy Spirit is the transaction of faith ("Forasmuch then as God gave them [Cornelius's household] the like gift, as he did unto us, who believed on the Lord Jesus Christ," Acts

11:17). These two contexts emphasize believers as the ones being baptized and teach that believers are baptized with the power of the Holy Spirit as a matter of fact when they believe on Jesus.

All six passages use the same exact phrase: *en Pneuma Hagias*, "with [the] Holy Ghost," meaning "with the power of the Holy Spirit." Therefore, this second direction of Spirit baptism primarily relates to Spirit empowerment. This great truth will be expanded later.

2. The implicit passages add a few more details. First Corinthians 12:13 implies that the second direction of Spirit baptism occurs in conjunction with the first direction: "For by one Spirit are we all baptized into one body, whether we be Jews or Gentiles, whether we be bond or free; and have been all made to drink into one Spirit." The first phrase of this verse is always cited as the proof text for being baptized *into* Christ. But the last phrase is often overlooked, perhaps because the middle phrases form a parenthesis of thought. However, the last phrase describes, rather than explicitly states, being baptized *with* the Spirit: "and have been all made to drink into one Spirit." This context teaches that when believers are baptized into the body of Christ, they are also baptized with the Holy Spirit.

Galatians 3:26–27 also implies the second direction of Spirit baptism occurs in conjunction with the first direction, reveals the timing of both directions of Spirit baptism more clearly, and emphasizes a parallel phrase that describes being baptized with the Holy Spirit: "For ye are all the children of God by faith in Christ Jesus. For as many of you as have been baptized into Christ have put on Christ." The next verse explains that there is neither Jew nor Greek, bond nor free, male nor female, since all are "one in Christ Jesus," making this passage parallel to First Corinthians 12:13. Just as First Corinthians 12:13 does not stop by simply stating that believers are baptized *into* Christ but also describes believers as being baptized *with* the Spirit, so Galatians 3:27 does not stop by simply stating believers "have been baptized *into* Christ" but also describes believers as being baptized *with* the Spirit in the words "have put on Christ." The timing of both directions of Spirit baptism is the moment of faith for salvation ("by faith . . . For as many of you as have been baptized into Christ have put on Christ"). The words "have put on" are translated from the Greek word *enduo*; it means "clothed with" or "invested with" and is found in Luke 24:49: "be endued with power from on high." This phrase in Luke exactly parallels one in Acts 1:5, "be baptized with the Holy Ghost," since both phrases describe what the believers were to "tarry" or "wait" for in Jerusalem prior to Pentecost. Inspiration, therefore, makes the phraseology of the second direction of Spirit baptism *baptized with* parallel to the phrase "endued with." Being "baptized with Holy Spirit-ness" is the same as being "*endued with* power from on high." This enduement largely conveys the idea of the Spirit coming "upon" someone for service (as, for example, in Luke 4:18 and Acts 1:8). This context also teaches when believers are baptized into Christ, they are baptized with Christ, which is the idea of being invested with the power of Christ in them—the Holy Spirit.

In summary, the second direction of Spirit baptism is being baptized by the Son *with* the Spirit. The agent who baptizes is Christ, the ones being baptized are believers, the description of what believers are baptized with is the power of the Holy Spirit, the means of the baptism is faith, and the timing of this direction of Spirit baptism is the transaction of faith for salvation. When believers are baptized *into* Christ, they are baptized *with* the Spirit.

To summarize all the facts noted thus far regarding the baptism of the Holy Spirit, there is one baptism with two directions. At salvation the Holy Spirit baptizes the believer *into* Christ, and Christ baptizes the believer *with* the Holy Spirit. Ten contexts unfold this conclusion. Four addressed the first direction and eight the second, two of which also addressed the first. The Gospel accounts pointed forward prophetically to the coming age of Spirit baptism, the contexts in Acts recorded the inauguration of this age, and the Epistles then explained that Spirit baptism occurs as a matter of fact when believers exercise saving faith.

Two Directions: Two Provisions

The fact of one baptism with two directions is foundational to the fact that the two directions represent two provisions.

1. *The Believer in Christ:* The first provision of Spirit baptism is the direct result of being baptized by the Spirit *into* Christ: "you in Christ." The believer has a new position—identification *in Christ*. The "in Christ" phrase, including its several equivalents, occurs at least 242 times in the New Testament, 216 of which occur in the Epistles—a remarkable emphasis. This is the provision of "entitlement."

The most significant context as to the provision of this new position is Ephesians 1–2. Ephesians 1:3 states that saints are blessed "with all spiritual blessings in heavenly places *in Christ.*" Ephesians 1:19–2:6 describes the display of God's power:

> He raised him [Christ] from the dead, and set him at his own right hand in the heavenly places, Far above all principality, and power, and might, and dominion, and every name that is named. . . . And hath raised us up together, and made us to sit together in heavenly places *in Christ Jesus.* (1:20–21; 2:6)

Not only are believers identified with Christ in His death, burial and resurrection, they are identified with Christ in His throne seat far above the enemy. Since believers are *in Christ*, in the spirit realm, or "heavenly places," believers are as far above the powers of darkness as Christ is. This position of entitlement implies a divine authority. This is a marvelous position.

In Christ believers are blessed with a position of divine authority over the powers of darkness. This position of entitlement includes the provision of defense to protect against "all the fiery darts of the wicked" (Eph. 6:16) and the provision of offense for "the pulling down of strong holds" (2 Cor. 10:3–5). *In Christ* believers possess delegated authority to counterattack and overrule a defeated foe. This is a powerful provision.

2. *Christ in the Believer:* The second provision of Spirit baptism is the direct result of being baptized by the Son *with* the Spirit: "Christ in you." The believer has a new power—investment *with the Holy Spirit*. The Spirit of Christ moves into the believer to impart to him the victorious life of Jesus Christ. This allows the believer to be invested with, or clothed with, the Spirit of Christ. This is the provision of "enduement."

It has been noted that the phrase "be baptized with the Holy Spirit" (Acts 1:5), parallels contextually the phrase "be endued with power from on high" (Luke 24:49). As noted, the absence of the definite article "the" in the Greek of the first phrase emphasizes the quality of the person named. The emphasis of this second direction of Spirit baptism is being baptized with the power of the Holy Spirit and is equivalent conceptually to being "endued with power from on high." The word "power" (*dunamis*) means "ability," in this case "from on high." Both contexts reveal that the power of the Spirit is the dynamic needed to be "witnesses" in order to fulfill the Great Commission (Luke 24:48; Acts 1:8). Therefore, enduement pertains to divine ability. This is a glorious power.

The enduement of Christ in the believer includes three major emphases for one major purpose. These conclusions are based on the analogy of faith, comparing Scripture with Scripture regarding empowerment in the believer's life. Christ taught all three emphases in John 14–16 as a part of the coming ministry of the Holy Spirit. Acts records the inauguration of that ministry, and the Epistles then confirm these concepts.

First, there is the anointing of understanding pertaining to spiritual illumination. First John 2:20 says, "But ye have [are having] an *unction* [anointing] from the Holy One, and ye *know* [*oida*, are knowing] all things." First John 2:27 further declares, "But the *anointing* which ye have received of him abideth [is abiding] in you, and ye need not that any man teach you: but . . . *the same anointing teacheth* [is teaching] you of all things, and is truth, and is no lie." This anointing of understanding regarding the truth of God endues believers to preach the Word. Jesus Himself said, "The Spirit of the Lord is upon me, because he hath *anointed me to preach the gospel*" (Luke 4:18). The anointing of understanding is when one's mental faculties are invigorated through spiritual illumination of the grand realities of truth that connect to the words of God. The anointing of understanding is the enabling for "*knowing* right" or "*knowing* truth."

Second, there is the filling for holiness. Ephesians 5:18 commands the believer to "be filled with [the quality of] the Spirit" in the context of being what one ought to be in his relationships. Galatians 5:16 and 22–23 commands, promises and explains, "Walk in [the quality of] the Spirit, and ye shall not fulfill the lust of the flesh. . . . But the fruit of the Spirit is love, joy, peace, longsuffering, gentleness, goodness, faith, meekness, temperance." Both commands are structured in the original Greek to emphasize the quality of the Spirit. The filling for holiness is when one's personal being is infused with the holy life of Christ—His love and all the accompanying attributes. This is the Spirit-filled life for holiness—the Spirit imparting to the believer the holy life of Jesus Christ. The filling for holiness is the enabling for "*being* right" or "*living* truth."

Third, there is the overflowing for service. Jesus promised those who would believe that from their innermost being "shall flow rivers of living water . . . [the] Spirit" (John 7:38). Acts 1:8 states, "But ye shall receive power . . . and ye shall be witnesses." Acts 2:4 and 11 records: "And they were all filled with the Holy Ghost, and began to speak . . . the wonderful works of God." Acts 4:31 says, "And they were all filled with the Holy Ghost, and they spake the word of God with boldness." In fact, the concept of being filled and then witnessing occurs repeatedly throughout Acts. In each case when believers were "filled with the Holy Spirit," the filling overflowed into speaking truth. This might be termed "the fullness of the Spirit." The filling or overflowing for service is when one's communicating capacities are liberated to testify unashamedly of Jesus. This is the Spirit-filled life for service—the Spirit imparting to and through and even upon the believer the serving life of Jesus Christ. The overflowing for service is the enabling for "*doing* right" or "*speaking* truth."

Ultimately, all three emphases of the enduement are for the major purpose of communicating God's truth. Jesus said the Spirit was "upon" Him because He "anointed me to preach" (Luke 4:18). The illumined understanding is for truth proclamation. Even the filling for holiness command "be filled with the Spirit" is immediately followed with "Speaking . . . ." Holy living is for the purpose of effctive ministry to others. As seen in Acts, the Spirit came "upon" believers that they might be "witnesses" (Acts 1:8) and when believers were "filled with the Spirit" they "spake" with boldness (Acts 4:31). The enduement is the combination of all three emphases ulimately for service. The second direction of Spirit baptism emphasizes the provision of the power of Pentecost to fulfill the Great Commission.

With the Spirit (Christ in the believer) believers are blessed with the power of divine ability over the world and the flesh as well as power for service. This power of enduement, or "enduement of power," includes the provision of the anointing of understanding and the filling for holiness, both of which are for the overflowing for service. Since the Spirit imparts to the believer the knowledge of Christ, the holiness of Christ and the service of Christ, the enduement or second direction of Spirit baptism is in a real sense a revelation of Jesus Christ. It is the Spirit imparting to and through the believer the life of Christ. This is the Spirit-filled life—the Spirit filling and over-flowing the believer with the life of Christ. *With the Spirit* believers have access to divine ability to counteract and overcome the world and the flesh that they might engage in empowered service. This is a powerful provision.

To summarize the two provisions inherent in the two directions of Spirit baptism: being baptized by the Spirit *into* Christ provides the believer with the position of "you in Christ," and being baptized by the Son *with* the Spirit provides the believer with the power of "Christ in you." The former provision focuses on identification *in Christ*; the latter focuses on investment *with the Spirit*. The former is a matter of entitlement; the latter is a matter of enduement. The former entitles the believer to exercise divine authority in the spiritual realm; the latter endues the believer to access divine ability in the physical realm. These two provisions equip believers both with divine authority and divine ability ultimately to fulfill the Great Commission.

As an actual matter of fact, at salvation believers are baptized *into* Christ and *with* the Spirit, providing them with divine authority and divine ability. But many believers live far below their provision. How can the facts translate into function?

The Function

The facts demand faith to become functional in the believer's life. Although the baptism of the Holy Spirit is bestowed to the believer at salvation, there is a difference between what is factual and what is functional. A carpenter may factually possess tools for carpentry work, but he must depend on those tools by using them for the function of carpentry. Likewise, faith is the necessary link between the factual and the functional in the matter of Spirit baptism.

"But without faith it is impossible to please him [God]" (Heb. 11:6). Through Christ "we have access by faith into this grace wherein we stand" (Rom. 5:2). As a matter of fact, believers have been baptized *into* Christ and *with* the Spirit. But as a matter of function, believers must "access by faith" their provision, without which it is impossible to please God.

Regarding the first direction of Spirit baptism that provides the entitlement of divine authority, Ephesians 1:19, in the context of the believer positioned in Christ at the throne seat, says, "And what is the exceeding greatness of his power to *us-ward who believe.*" The present tense of "believe" indicates continuous or repeated believing. Defensively, Ephesians 6:16 explains the "shield of faith" quenches or extinguishes "all the fiery darts of the wicked [one]." Any fiery dart from the unseen realm may be rejected authoritatively by faith as one claims his position in Christ at the throne. Offensively, by faith believers may take ground from the enemy that Christ won at the cross. Faith may access greater works (John 14:12), to pull down strongholds or deceptions of wrong thinking (2 Cor. 10:3–5), and allow the Word of God to have free course and its full weight on the hearts of hearers (2 Thess. 3:1).

As an actual matter of fact, believers are entitled to exercise divine authority. But as a matter of function, they must exercise that authority by faith. Faith then turns the facts into function.

Regarding the second direction of Spirit baptism that provides the enduement of divine ability, faith again is the key that unlocks the facts into function. According to Galatians 3:27, the fact is that believers "have put on [been endued with] Christ." This verb phrase is in the indicative mood, which is the mood of reality. Yet Romans 13:14 admonishes believers to "put ye on [be endued with] the Lord Jesus Christ." Here the verb phrase is in the imperative mood, which is the mood of potential. Why does Romans command what Galatians already claims? The answer lies in the truth that one must access by faith what *is* (factual) regarding the baptism of the Holy Spirit in order for it to be *experienced* (functional). The middle voice of the imperative indicates the believer is responsible to initiate the action through the choice of faith and then participate in the results.

Factually, one has been baptized or endued with the power of the Holy Spirit when he believed for salvation. This is a matter of objective reality. But functionally, one is baptized or endued with the power of the Holy Spirit repeatedly when he believes for Spirit-enabled living. This is a matter of subjective reality, as objective reality is then experienced. This dynamic is not a second blessing but a repeated access of one's first blessing. But if one has not accessed his provision in Christ for a long time, when he does access by faith his provision after a nonfunctional period, it may seem like a second blessing. However, in actuality it is simply accessing the blessing provided in the Spirit baptism that occurred at salvation.

This distinction between fact and function helps to explain the historical confusion of terms regarding the baptism of the Holy Spirit. Moody and Torrey emphasized the functional aspect, while others have emphasized the factual. Yet both are true.

In fact, this double-sided emphasis helps also to explain the historical terminology *experimental religion*. The word "experimental" was used not to discover if something was true but to demonstrate it was already true. Again, the burden was turning facts into function or objective reality into subjective reality.

As noted earlier, the enduement is the second direction of Spirit baptism, involving being baptized by the Son *with* the Spirit. This enduement of power includes the anointing of understanding, the filling for holiness and the overflowing for service, which together comprise the Spirit coming *upon* a believer for service. Many use the terminology "one baptism, many fillings." This is accurate and perhaps the best terminology to keep from being misunderstood. But when focusing solely on the second direction of Spirit baptism, it is also technically accurate to say "one baptism, many baptisms." One baptism referring to the factual ("have put on/been endued") and many baptisms referring to the functional ("put ye on/be endued"). This accounts for the many saints of God in the past who felt free to cry out to God for a "fresh baptism."

Regardless of the terminology one emphasizes, the point is that faith is necessary to access the facts into function. Galatians 3:5 clarifies this: "He therefore that ministereth [lit., is supplying] to you the Spirit, and worketh miracles among you, doeth he it by the works of the law, or by the hearing of faith?" Faith accesses fresh supplies of the ministry of the Holy Spirit as needed.

When the anointing of understanding is needed, believers may appropriate the anointing of the Spirit for illumination since "ye have [are having] an unction [anointing] from the Holy One, and ye know [are knowing] all things . . . the same anointing teacheth [is teaching] you of all things" (1 John 2:20, 27). Because the Spirit "is teaching" you, not "will teach," the simple steps of faith are only *take* and *act*. As the believer takes the Spirit's anointing to act on that reality, the Spirit illuminates the understanding.

When the filling for holiness is needed, believers may appropriate the life of Christ in them to be what they ought to be since "I live; yet not I, but Christ liveth in me" by "faith" (Gal. 2:20). Because Christ already lives in the believer, not "will live," the simple steps of faith are only *take* and *act*. As the believer takes Christ's patience, love, purity and so forth, and then acts upon that reality, the Spirit of Christ infuses the believer with Christ's victorious life.

When the overflowing for service is needed, believers may "ask" for the power of the Spirit, and the Father promises to "give" that enabling for service (Luke 11:13). Then believers may "receive" or "take" the provision and "be witnesses" (Acts 1:8). Therefore, the simple steps of faith are to *ask*, *take* and then *act,* trusting God to fulfill His promise of enabling for service. As the believer trusts to obey, the Holy Spirit empowers the believer to speak freely the gospel of Jesus Christ.

Notice that the provision of the anointing of understanding and the filling for holiness are both stated scripturally as present realities—facts. Therefore, they need not be asked for, they simply need to be appropriated through the faith-steps of taking and acting. However, the provision of the overflowing for service is stated scripturally as future potentialities—promises. Therefore, the faith-steps begin with asking, followed by taking (as God gives it), and then acting on it.

In summary, the Spirit teaching you (anointing of understanding) and Christ living in you (filling for holiness) are present realites, but must be appropriated by faith to be functional or manifest. On the other hand, the power of the Spirit on you for others (overflowing for service) is a future potentiality, but must also be accessed by faith to be functional.

As an actual matter of fact, believers are endued with divine ability. But as a matter of function, they must access that ability by faith. Faith then translates the facts into function. Whether focusing on the believer's position or power, faith is the victory.

The faith-filled believer who has learned to access his provision in Christ—divine authority and divine ability—may also then proceed to be an intercessor, seeking the outpouring of the Spirit for those who will not seek God's reviving presence on their own. But that is another subject.

The diagram below pictures Spirit baptism as an umbrella term.

	One Baptism				
Two Directions	▲ By the Spirit into Christ		▼ By the Son with the Spirit		
Two Provisions	Position: "You in Christ" Entitlement: Divine Authority		Power: "Christ in You" Enduement: Divine Ability		
	Defense	Offense	Anointing of Under-standing	Filling for Holiness	Overflowing for Service
Access	Faith				

The baptism of the Holy Spirit is one baptism with two directions, representing two provisions accessible by faith in order to be functional. The baptism *of* the Holy Spirit is a baptism *into* Christ and *with* the Spirit. It involves both what is a matter of fact once one is saved as the foundation for faith, and it involves what is a matter of function following one's salvation for the rest of his earthly days through the exercise of faith. Since the baptism of the Holy Spirit is both a glorious reality and a provisional potential for every believer, believers must depend upon the facts and by faith access the function of the baptism of the Holy Spirit. May every believer fully experience the reality of the baptism of the Holy Spirit, and therefore, fully experience *the Christ life*.

The combination of accessing divine authority to pull down strongholds with accessing divine ability to understand truth, live truth and ultimately to declare truth, form an amazing supernatural dynamic—the power of Pentecost to fulfill the Great Commission. This is *the revived life*. Will you by faith access the revived life to fulfill all God has for you?

Prayer

Dear Father, thank You that I have been baptized into Christ and with the Spirit. Grant that I may know this baptism experimentally to the fullest. Thank You for the entitlement privileges of throne seat authority both defensively and offensively. Thank You for the enduement of power. Therefore, I thank You, Lord, for the anointing of understanding and the filling for holiness. I trust You, Lord, to manifest these provisions. Also, I ask for the overflowing for service, and I take You, Lord, at Your Word to give Holy Spirit-ness to those who ask. O Lord, thank You for this blessing, and thank You for Your work in me and through me this day. Amen.

• • • • •

Questions for Personal Reflection

1. What facts has the Spirit made clear to you in this study?

2. In what ways has the Spirit impressed you to apply faith in order to turn facts into function?

3. How have you begun to experience the glorious freedom of Christ's life?

APPENDIX

Diagram A

The Unregenerated Condition: Dead to God and Alive to Sin
(Chapter 3)

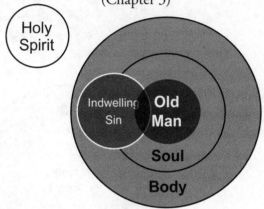

Diagram B

Death With Christ Unto Sin: Separation from Indwelling Sin
(Chapter 3)

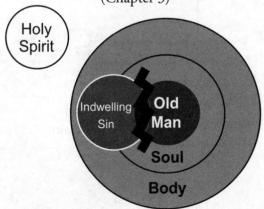

Diagram C
The Regenerated Condition:
Dead to Sin and
Alive to God (Chapter 3)

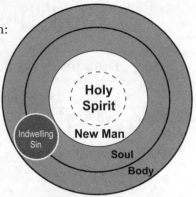

Diagram D
The Overcoming Life:
Christ to You (Chapter 6)

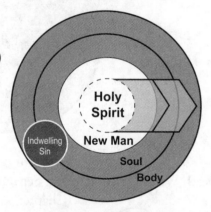

Diagram E
The Overflowing Life:
Christ through You
to Others (Chapter 7)

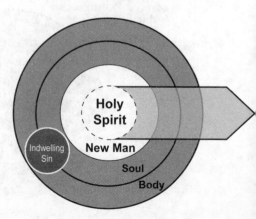

ENDNOTES

1. Dr. & Mrs. Howard Taylor, *Hudson Taylor and the China Inland Mission*, vol. 2 (Singapore: Overseas Missionary Fellowship, 1918, 1989), 163.

2. Ibid., 164–170 (emphasis original).

3. Ibid., 171.

4. Rosalind Goforth, *Climbing: Memories of a Missionary's Wife* (Nappanee, IN: Evangel Publishing House, 1940, 2008), 37–38.

5. Ibid., 45–46 (emphasis original).

6. Ibid., 179–180.

7. I.R. Govan, *The Spirit of Revival* (Edinburgh: The Faith Mission, 1938, 4th ed. 1978), 23–25.

8. Taylor, 168–177.

9. Andrew A. Woolsey, *Channel of Revival: A Biography of Duncan Campbell* (Edinburgh: The Faith Mission, 1974, 1982), 134–135.

10. The main thoughts in this section have been adapted from Adrian Rogers, *Kingdom Authority* (Nashville: Thomas Nelson, 2002), 34–42.

11. Ruth Paxson, *The Wealth, Walk, and Warfare of the Christian* (New York: Fleming H. Revell, 1939), 17.

12. Ibid., 58.

13. John MacMillan, *The Authority of the Believer* (Camp Hill, PA: WingSpread Publishers, 1981, 2007), 4.

14. Ibid., 38–39.

15. John Van Gelderen, unpublished chorus.

16. W.E. Boardman, *The Higher Christian Life* (Fort Washington, PA: CLC Publications, 1958, 2007), 62 (emphasis original).

17. Ibid., 73.

18. Ibid., 77 (emphasis original).

19. John Pollock, *The Cambridge Seven* (Leicester, UK: Inter-Varsity Press, 1955, 1996), 72–73 (emphasis original).

20. John Van Gelderen, *The Faith Response* (Fort Washington, PA: CLC Publications, 2011), 35 (emphasis original).

21. The Greek word *en* may be translated "in," "with" or "by." However, it is of great significance the more conservative translations have opted for the translation "with" in the explicit passages here mentioned. In fact, the KJV, NKJV, NIV and ESV all translate *en* as "with" in all six contexts. The NASB does as well except for John 1:33.

BIBLIOGRAPHY

Boardman, W.E. *The Higher Christian Life*. Fort Washington, PA: CLC Publications, 1958, 2007.

Goforth, Rosalind. *Climbing: Memories of a Missionary's Wife*. Nappanee, IN: Evangel Publishing, 1940, 2008.

Govan, I.R. *The Spirit of Revival*. Edinburgh, UK: The Faith Mission, 1938, 4th ed. 1978.

✓MacMillan, John. *The Authority of the Believer*. Camp Hill, PA: WingSpread, 1981, 2007.

Paxson, Ruth. *The Wealth, Walk, and Warfare of the Christian*. New York: Revell, 1939.

Pollock, John. *The Cambridge Seven*. Leicester, UK: Inter-Varsity Press, 1955, 1996.

✓Rogers, Adrian. *Kingdom Authority*. Nashville: Thomas Nelson, 2002.

Taylor, Dr. and Mrs. Howard. *Hudson Taylor and the China Inland Mission*, vol. 2. Singapore: Overseas Missionary Fellowship, 1918, 1989.

Woolsey, Andrew A. *Channel of Revival: A Biography of Duncan Campbell*. Edinburgh, UK: The Faith Mission, 1974, 1982.

PUBLICATIONS

Fort Washington, PA 19034

This book is published by CLC Publications, an outreach of CLC Ministries International. The purpose of CLC is to make evangelical Christian literature available to all nations so that people may come to faith and maturity in the Lord Jesus Christ. We hope this book has been life changing and has enriched your walk with God through the work of the Holy Spirit. If you would like to know more about CLC, we invite you to visit our website:

www.clcusa.org

To know more about the remarkable story of the founding of CLC International we encourage you to read

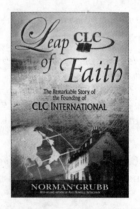

LEAP OF FAITH

Norman Grubb

Paperback
Size 5¹/₄ x 8, Pages 248
ISBN: 978-0-87508-650-7
ISBN (*e-book*): 978-1-61958-055-8